FOOD52

COOK
IN THE
BLANK

THE FUN, FREEWHEELING GAME PLAN
THAT TAKES YOU FROM ZERO TO DINNER

CLARKSON POTTER/PUBLISHERS

NEW YORK

Published in the United States by Clarkson Potter/Publishers,
an imprint of the Crown Publishing Group, a division of
Penguin Random House LLC, New York.
crownpublishing.com
clarksonpotter.com

CLARKSON POTTER is a trademark and POTTER with
colophon is a registered trademark of Penguin Random
House LLC.

ISBN 978-0-525-57445-3

Printed in China

Writing and recipe development by Rémy Robert
Illustrations by Tim McSweeney
Book design by Jen Wang

2 4 6 8 10 9 7 5 3 1

First Edition

COOK IN THE BLANK

Whether you're a by-the-books cook who measures life in teaspoons or a fly-by-the-seat-of-your-pants chef who chops now and thinks later, you're probably going to eat dinner tonight. There are times for illustrious feasts and times for takeout—and then there are all the nights in between. Nights when you're eager to use up whatever's kicking around in your crisper, nights when you're on the hook for feeding your potluck or book club. Not to mention nights when it's too cold or too late to leave the house . . . or when it's Monday.

Cook in the Blank is for all those nights. Dinnertime can be an adventure, and now you get to design your own. The twenty recipes that follow lay the groundwork for effortless cooking, giving you a little structure where you need it and a world of freedom everywhere else. Leaf through and you'll see something akin to recipes, save for the gaps peppered throughout each set of instructions. Those aren't typos—they're invitations for you to ad-lib, interchange, give in to whims, and let inspiration (or necessity) take over. Fill them in as you see fit, and voilà—you've put together a fully functional recipe that is completely yours. You'll find each recipe three times so that you can try a few different spins or share them around.

Use these templates to become your own mealtime hero, or play them as a game with your kids, spouse, roommate, or zany neighbor. The results are likely to be both delicious and fun. These are meals that you can fearlessly adapt to your mood and pantry, that you can juggle when there are a dozen other items on your to-do list. Maybe, for you, this sounds like a pot of soup. Or burgers. Or a frittata. As it turns out, you don't need to be a seasoned home cook or pro chef to cook without a recipe. You just need a little inspiration (and to like eating).

Cook in the Blank is playful, forgiving, and subject to all your wacky whims. Within these pages, you'll find the guardrails for bold experimentation—as well as permission to put dinner on cruise control. Either way, you've got this.

HOW TO PLAY

FILL IN THE BLANKS. Grab a pencil—or a pen, if you're feeling bold—and cobble together a game plan, one blank at a time. (At a loss? Peep at the sample on the next page to help break the ice.)

USE WHAT YOU HAVE. The first step to making dinner easier is to look at what's in front of you. If you've got a container of leftovers or a new ingredient you're excited to use, spin the rest off that. Otherwise, peruse your pantry to see what you can pull together before you book it to the grocery store.

COOK WHAT YOU LIKE. Your kitchen, your rules. The best meals come from what you like best, so stock up on spices that smell wonderful, produce that calls out to you, or whatever looks good at the butcher or fishmonger.

CROWDSOURCE IT. Poll your family and friends to fill the blanks. Welcome special requests, or let your little ones choose the menu for a night.

PICK A THEME AND RUN WITH IT. If you're looking for structure or guidance, stick with a cuisine (say, cumin, chiles, and black beans for something Mexican-influenced), a mood (stick-to-your-ribs, light-and-bright), or even a color or a season.

LOOK TO THE HINTS AND WINKS. On the back of each recipe you'll find a slew of ideas, from practical to silly, for all the components of your next meal. Use them as a springboard for filling in the blanks, but also . . .

. . . GO OFF SCRIPT. If you have an idea but don't see it in the suggestions, go rogue. Can't decide which protein or grain to use? Go with a combo!

TAKE NOTES ALONG THE WAY. If you've tried something and struck gold, write it down so you remember it. There's a blank section on the back of each template where you can scrawl your lessons, hopes, and dreams. Consider it a down payment on future dinners.

Our cooking victories are meant to be shared and nurtured, so when you hit on something you love, invite it to stay in your kitchen. Tear it out of the book to file away with your other back-pocket dinners, pass it along at your next recipe swap, or send a copy off to your mom or best friend. Let *Cook in the Blank* inspire you to try something you've never had before. Who knows, you just might pave the path to your next famous chili, salad, roast chicken—or fill in the blank!

BUBBLING BAKED _rigatoni_

PASTA

WITH _caramelized onions_ & _cheddar_ CHEESE

ADDED OOHS & AHHS · TYPE OF CHEESE

① Preheat the oven to 400°F. Grease a rectangular baking dish with any type of cooking fat.

② Bring a large pot of very salty water to a boil. Add 1 pound ___rigatoni___

PASTA

and cook until it's al dente (not completely tender, but close to it). Drain it.

③ While the pasta cooks, grate a few cups of ___Cheddar___ cheese into a

TYPE OF CHEESE

big bowl. (The more cheese, the meltier your dinner.) Add a few glugs of

___heavy cream___ , a few dashes of ___Dijon mustard___ , and some

DAIRY · SEASONINGS

___goat___ cheese if you're looking for extra flavor.

FUNKIER CHEESE

④ Fold in a few heaps of chopped ___kale___ and some

GREENS

___caramelized onions___ , if you want—or skip it all and stick to the pasta-and-

ADDED OOHS & AHHS

cheese classic.

⑤ Mix in the drained cooked pasta, then pour the whole mess into the greased baking dish

(or go with a sheet pan for more crispy bits, tops, and edges, if you like). Cover it with

___buttery bread crumbs___ , more cheese, and/or ___smoked sea salt___ .

SOMETHING THAT'LL GET CRUNCHY · SOMETHING OVER THE TOP

⑥ Turn on ___Burnt Toast___ and bake your pasta for 30 to 45 minutes.

YOUR FAVORITE PODCAST

Remove it from the oven when it's bubbling and golden brown. Serve yourself a heaping

scoop and count to at least 10 Mississippi before taking a bite.

—SAMPLE—

BUBBLING BAKED _____
PASTA

WITH _____ & _____ CHEESE
ADDED OOHS & AHHS TYPE OF CHEESE

① Preheat the oven to 400°F. Grease a rectangular baking dish with any type of cooking fat.

② Bring a large pot of very salty water to a boil. Add 1 pound _____
PASTA

and cook until it's al dente (not completely tender, but close to it). Drain it.

③ While the pasta cooks, grate a few cups of _____ cheese into a
TYPE OF CHEESE

big bowl. (The more cheese, the meltier your dinner.) Add a few glugs of

_____ , a few dashes of _____ , and some
DAIRY SEASONINGS

_____ cheese if you're looking for extra flavor.
FUNKIER CHEESE

④ Fold in a few heaps of chopped _____ and some
GREENS

_____ , if you want—or skip it all and stick to the pasta-and-
ADDED OOHS & AHHS

cheese classic.

⑤ Mix in the drained cooked pasta, then pour the whole mess into the greased baking dish

(or go with a sheet pan for more crispy bits, tops, and edges, if you like). Cover it with

_____ , more cheese, and/or _____ .
SOMETHING THAT'LL GET CRUNCHY SOMETHING OVER THE TOP

⑥ Turn on _____ and bake your pasta for 30 to 45 minutes.
YOUR FAVORITE PODCAST

Remove it from the oven when it's bubbling and golden brown. Serve yourself a heaping

scoop and count to at least 10 Mississippi before taking a bite.

HINTS AND WINKS

PASTA
- cavatelli
- macaroni
- rigatoni
- conchiglie
- fusilli

ADDED OOHS & AHHS
- sautéed mushrooms
- caramelized onions
- pulled pork
- cooked bacon
- crabmeat or lobster

TYPE OF CHEESE
- cheddar
- mozzarella
- Gruyère
- fontina
- Manchego

DAIRY
- milk
- heavy cream
- half-and-half

SEASONINGS
- Dijon mustard
- paprika
- cayenne
- hot sauce
- dried oregano

FUNKIER CHEESE
- blue
- crumbled goat
- robiola

GREENS
- kale
- mustard or collard greens
- spinach

SOMETHING THAT'LL GET CRUNCHY
- panko
- pine nuts
- cubed white or sourdough bread
- **Buttery Bread Crumbs**

SOMETHING OVER THE TOP
- sliced prosciutto
- diced pepperoni
- truffle oil
- smoked sea salt
- diamonds

YOUR FAVORITE PODCAST
- *Burnt Toast*
- *This American Life*
- *How Did This Get Made?*
- *Serial*

WHIP IT UP

BUTTERY BREAD CRUMBS

Blitz some crusty—and preferably stale—bread to smithereens in a food processor. For every ½ cup crumbs, add **1 to 2 tablespoons melted butter**. You can also stir in **¼ cup grated Parmesan or pecorino cheese** and **2 tablespoons chopped fresh herbs**. Sprinkle the mixture over your pasta before you bake it, or toast it all together in a skillet and serve over roasted vegetables or a hearty salad. (Or eat it with a spoon.)

NOTES TO YOUR FUTURE SELF

BUBBLING BAKED _____
PASTA

WITH _____ & _____ CHEESE
ADDED OOHS & AHHS   TYPE OF CHEESE

① Preheat the oven to 400°F. Grease a rectangular baking dish with any type of cooking fat.

② Bring a large pot of very salty water to a boil. Add 1 pound _____
PASTA

and cook until it's al dente (not completely tender, but close to it). Drain it.

③ While the pasta cooks, grate a few cups of _____ cheese into a
TYPE OF CHEESE

big bowl. (The more cheese, the meltier your dinner.) Add a few glugs of

_____ , a few dashes of _____ , and some
DAIRY   SEASONINGS

_____ cheese if you're looking for extra flavor.
FUNKIER CHEESE

④ Fold in a few heaps of chopped _____ and some
GREENS

_____ , if you want—or skip it all and stick to the pasta-and-
ADDED OOHS & AHHS

cheese classic.

⑤ Mix in the drained cooked pasta, then pour the whole mess into the greased baking dish

(or go with a sheet pan for more crispy bits, tops, and edges, if you like). Cover it with

_____ , more cheese, and/or _____ .
SOMETHING THAT'LL GET CRUNCHY   SOMETHING OVER THE TOP

⑥ Turn on _____ and bake your pasta for 30 to 45 minutes.
YOUR FAVORITE PODCAST

Remove it from the oven when it's bubbling and golden brown. Serve yourself a heaping

scoop and count to at least 10 Mississippi before taking a bite.

HINTS AND WINKS

PASTA
- cavatelli
- macaroni
- rigatoni
- conchiglie
- fusilli

ADDED OOHS & AHHS
- sautéed mushrooms
- caramelized onions
- pulled pork
- cooked bacon
- crabmeat or lobster

TYPE OF CHEESE
- cheddar
- mozzarella
- Gruyère
- fontina
- Manchego

DAIRY
- milk
- heavy cream
- half-and-half

SEASONINGS
- Dijon mustard
- paprika
- cayenne
- hot sauce
- dried oregano

FUNKIER CHEESE
- blue
- crumbled goat
- robiola

GREENS
- kale
- mustard or collard greens
- spinach

SOMETHING THAT'LL GET CRUNCHY
- panko
- pine nuts
- cubed white or sourdough bread
- **Buttery Bread Crumbs**

SOMETHING OVER THE TOP
- sliced prosciutto
- diced pepperoni
- truffle oil
- smoked sea salt
- diamonds

YOUR FAVORITE PODCAST
- *Burnt Toast*
- *This American Life*
- *How Did This Get Made?*
- *Serial*

WHIP IT UP

BUTTERY BREAD CRUMBS

Blitz some crusty—and preferably stale—bread to smithereens in a food processor. For every ½ cup crumbs, add **1 to 2 tablespoons melted butter**. You can also stir in ¼ **cup grated Parmesan or pecorino cheese** and **2 tablespoons chopped fresh herbs**. Sprinkle the mixture over your pasta before you bake it, or toast it all together in a skillet and serve over roasted vegetables or a hearty salad. (Or eat it with a spoon.)

NOTES TO YOUR FUTURE SELF

_____

_____

_____

_____

_____

BUBBLING BAKED _____
PASTA

WITH _____ & _____ CHEESE
ADDED OOHS & AHHS   TYPE OF CHEESE

① Preheat the oven to 400°F. Grease a rectangular baking dish with any type of cooking fat.

② Bring a large pot of very salty water to a boil. Add 1 pound _____
PASTA

and cook until it's al dente (not completely tender, but close to it). Drain it.

③ While the pasta cooks, grate a few cups of _____ cheese into a
TYPE OF CHEESE

big bowl. (The more cheese, the meltier your dinner.) Add a few glugs of

_____ , a few dashes of _____ , and some
DAIRY   SEASONINGS

_____ cheese if you're looking for extra flavor.
FUNKIER CHEESE

④ Fold in a few heaps of chopped _____ and some
GREENS

_____ , if you want—or skip it all and stick to the pasta-and-
ADDED OOHS & AHHS

cheese classic.

⑤ Mix in the drained cooked pasta, then pour the whole mess into the greased baking dish

(or go with a sheet pan for more crispy bits, tops, and edges, if you like). Cover it with

_____ , more cheese, and/or _____ .
SOMETHING THAT'LL GET CRUNCHY   SOMETHING OVER THE TOP

⑥ Turn on _____ and bake your pasta for 30 to 45 minutes.
YOUR FAVORITE PODCAST

Remove it from the oven when it's bubbling and golden brown. Serve yourself a heaping

scoop and count to at least 10 Mississippi before taking a bite.

HINTS AND WINKS

PASTA
- cavatelli
- macaroni
- rigatoni
- conchiglie
- fusilli

ADDED OOHS & AHHS
- sautéed mushrooms
- caramelized onions
- pulled pork
- cooked bacon
- crabmeat or lobster

TYPE OF CHEESE
- cheddar
- mozzarella
- Gruyère
- fontina
- Manchego

DAIRY
- milk
- heavy cream
- half-and-half

SEASONINGS
- Dijon mustard
- paprika
- cayenne
- hot sauce
- dried oregano

FUNKIER CHEESE
- blue
- crumbled goat
- robiola

GREENS
- kale
- mustard or collard greens
- spinach

SOMETHING THAT'LL GET CRUNCHY
- panko
- pine nuts
- cubed white or sourdough bread
- **Buttery Bread Crumbs**

SOMETHING OVER THE TOP
- sliced prosciutto
- diced pepperoni
- truffle oil
- smoked sea salt
- diamonds

YOUR FAVORITE PODCAST
- *Burnt Toast*
- *This American Life*
- *How Did This Get Made?*
- *Serial*

WHIP IT UP

BUTTERY BREAD CRUMBS

Blitz some crusty—and preferably stale—bread to smithereens in a food processor. For every ½ cup crumbs, add **1 to 2 tablespoons melted butter**. You can also stir in **¼ cup grated Parmesan or pecorino cheese** and **2 tablespoons chopped fresh herbs**. Sprinkle the mixture over your pasta before you bake it, or toast it all together in a skillet and serve over roasted vegetables or a hearty salad. (Or eat it with a spoon.)

NOTES TO YOUR FUTURE SELF

_____

_____

_____

_____

_____

_____'s _____
YOUR NAME   ADJECTIVE

ROAST CHICKEN DINNER

①   Preheat the oven to 400°F.

②   If a little _____ is in the cards, chop it up and get some
SOMETHING SAVORY

_____ warm in an ovenproof skillet over medium heat. Fry your
COOKING FAT

little something until it's crispy, then strain it out and set it aside.

③   Scatter a few cups of chopped _____ across a rimmed baking
STURDY VEGETABLES

sheet, then add some chopped _____ and up to 1 cup each of
ALLIUMS

_____ and _____ . Throw in a little
SOMETHING SWEETISH   MORE STUFF

_____ for good measure.
SOMETHING PEPPY

④   Season the whole pan with salt, a few teaspoons of _____ ,
SPICES

and a couple tablespoons of _____ , plus a drizzle of
LIQUID GOLD

_____ ; toss it all to combine. Tuck a few sprigs of
COOKING FAT

_____ in the middle of everything.
FRESH HERBS

⑤   Coat 1 to 2 pounds of bone-in, skin-on chicken pieces with a little more

_____ and rub them with _____ .
COOKING FAT   SOMETHING THAT'LL STICK

Nestle the chicken pieces over the vegetables, skin side up.

⑥   Roast for 20 to 30 minutes, until the chicken is cooked through. Its juices will have

rendered into the melee below, so scoop it all up with a big spoon and serve it topped

with the crispy little savory something and _____ .
SOMETHING TO FINISH

HINTS AND WINKS

ADJECTIVE
- miraculous
- easy
- spicy
- world-famous

SOMETHING SAVORY
- bacon or pancetta
- sausage

COOKING FAT
- olive oil
- butter
- schmaltz

STURDY VEGETABLES
- summer or winter squash
- carrots or parsnips
- potatoes
- cauliflower

ALLIUMS
- red or yellow onions
- shallots
- leeks
- garlic

SOMETHING SWEETISH
- grapes
- dried apricots
- cherry tomatoes

MORE STUFF
- torn or cubed bread
- cooked or canned chickpeas
- pitted olives
- capers
- sun-dried tomatoes

SOMETHING PEPPY
- lemon zest or slices
- orange wedges

SPICES
- jerk seasoning
- ground cumin or coriander
- paprika
- za'atar

LIQUID GOLD
- orange juice
- soy sauce
- balsamic vinegar
- red or white wine

FRESH HERBS
- thyme
- sage
- marjoram
- rosemary

SOMETHING THAT'LL STICK
- harissa
- fancy mustard
- brown sugar or maple syrup
- pomegranate molasses

SOMETHING TO FINISH
- feta
- torn fresh herbs
- yogurt sauce
- pesto or gremolata
- romesco

TIP

GOT LEFTOVERS?

Leftovers alone are reason enough to roast a pan of chicken and vegetables. Shred the extra meat and toss it and its vegetable brethren into your favorite **chopped salad** or **grain bowl,** build a **potpie** or **frittata** around them, or swirl them into a **soup** at the very end of cooking.

NOTES TO YOUR FUTURE SELF

_____

_____

_____

_____

_____

_____

_____'s _____
YOUR NAME   ADJECTIVE

ROAST CHICKEN DINNER

① Preheat the oven to 400°F.

② If a little _____ is in the cards, chop it up and get some
            SOMETHING SAVORY

_____ warm in an ovenproof skillet over medium heat. Fry your
        COOKING FAT

little something until it's crispy, then strain it out and set it aside.

③ Scatter a few cups of chopped _____ across a rimmed baking
                                STURDY VEGETABLES

sheet, then add some chopped _____ and up to 1 cup each of
                            ALLIUMS

_____ and _____ . Throw in a little
    SOMETHING SWEETISH   MORE STUFF

_____ for good measure.
    SOMETHING PEPPY

④ Season the whole pan with salt, a few teaspoons of _____ ,
                                                    SPICES

and a couple tablespoons of _____ , plus a drizzle of
                            LIQUID GOLD

_____ ; toss it all to combine. Tuck a few sprigs of
    COOKING FAT

_____ in the middle of everything.
    FRESH HERBS

⑤ Coat 1 to 2 pounds of bone-in, skin-on chicken pieces with a little more

_____ and rub them with _____ .
    COOKING FAT   SOMETHING THAT'LL STICK

Nestle the chicken pieces over the vegetables, skin side up.

⑥ Roast for 20 to 30 minutes, until the chicken is cooked through. Its juices will have

rendered into the melee below, so scoop it all up with a big spoon and serve it topped

with the crispy little savory something and _____ .
                                            SOMETHING TO FINISH

HINTS AND WINKS

ADJECTIVE
- miraculous
- easy
- spicy
- world-famous

SOMETHING SAVORY
- bacon or pancetta
- sausage

COOKING FAT
- olive oil
- butter
- schmaltz

STURDY VEGETABLES
- summer or winter squash
- carrots or parsnips
- potatoes
- cauliflower

ALLIUMS
- red or yellow onions
- shallots
- leeks
- garlic

SOMETHING SWEETISH
- grapes
- dried apricots
- cherry tomatoes

MORE STUFF
- torn or cubed bread
- cooked or canned chickpeas
- pitted olives
- capers
- sun-dried tomatoes

SOMETHING PEPPY
- lemon zest or slices
- orange wedges

SPICES
- jerk seasoning
- ground cumin or coriander
- paprika
- za'atar

LIQUID GOLD
- orange juice
- soy sauce
- balsamic vinegar
- red or white wine

FRESH HERBS
- thyme
- sage
- marjoram
- rosemary

SOMETHING THAT'LL STICK
- harissa
- fancy mustard
- brown sugar or maple syrup
- pomegranate molasses

SOMETHING TO FINISH
- feta
- torn fresh herbs
- yogurt sauce
- pesto or gremolata
- romesco

TIP

GOT LEFTOVERS?

Leftovers alone are reason enough to roast a pan of chicken and vegetables. Shred the extra meat and toss it and its vegetable brethren into your favorite **chopped salad** or **grain bowl,** build a **potpie** or **frittata** around them, or swirl them into a **soup** at the very end of cooking.

NOTES TO YOUR FUTURE SELF

_____'s _____
YOUR NAME   ADJECTIVE

ROAST CHICKEN DINNER

① Preheat the oven to 400°F.

② If a little _____ is in the cards, chop it up and get some
SOMETHING SAVORY

_____ warm in an ovenproof skillet over medium heat. Fry your
COOKING FAT

little something until it's crispy, then strain it out and set it aside.

③ Scatter a few cups of chopped _____ across a rimmed baking
STURDY VEGETABLES

sheet, then add some chopped _____ and up to 1 cup each of
ALLIUMS

_____ and _____ . Throw in a little
SOMETHING SWEETISH   MORE STUFF

_____ for good measure.
SOMETHING PEPPY

④ Season the whole pan with salt, a few teaspoons of _____ ,
SPICES

and a couple tablespoons of _____ , plus a drizzle of
LIQUID GOLD

_____ ; toss it all to combine. Tuck a few sprigs of
COOKING FAT

_____ in the middle of everything.
FRESH HERBS

⑤ Coat 1 to 2 pounds of bone-in, skin-on chicken pieces with a little more

_____ and rub them with _____ .
COOKING FAT   SOMETHING THAT'LL STICK

Nestle the chicken pieces over the vegetables, skin side up.

⑥ Roast for 20 to 30 minutes, until the chicken is cooked through. Its juices will have

rendered into the melee below, so scoop it all up with a big spoon and serve it topped

with the crispy little savory something and _____ .
SOMETHING TO FINISH

HINTS AND WINKS

ADJECTIVE
- miraculous
- easy
- spicy
- world-famous

SOMETHING SAVORY
- bacon or pancetta
- sausage

COOKING FAT
- olive oil
- butter
- schmaltz

STURDY VEGETABLES
- summer or winter squash
- carrots or parsnips
- potatoes
- cauliflower

ALLIUMS
- red or yellow onions
- shallots
- leeks
- garlic

SOMETHING SWEETISH
- grapes
- dried apricots
- cherry tomatoes

MORE STUFF
- torn or cubed bread
- cooked or canned chickpeas
- pitted olives
- capers
- sun-dried tomatoes

SOMETHING PEPPY
- lemon zest or slices
- orange wedges

SPICES
- jerk seasoning
- ground cumin or coriander
- paprika
- za'atar

LIQUID GOLD
- orange juice
- soy sauce
- balsamic vinegar
- red or white wine

FRESH HERBS
- thyme
- sage
- marjoram
- rosemary

SOMETHING THAT'LL STICK
- harissa
- fancy mustard
- brown sugar or maple syrup
- pomegranate molasses

SOMETHING TO FINISH
- feta
- torn fresh herbs
- yogurt sauce
- pesto or gremolata
- romesco

TIP

GOT LEFTOVERS?

Leftovers alone are reason enough to roast a pan of chicken and vegetables. Shred the extra meat and toss it and its vegetable brethren into your favorite **chopped salad** or **grain bowl,** build a **potpie** or **frittata** around them, or swirl them into a **soup** at the very end of cooking.

NOTES TO YOUR FUTURE SELF

_____

_____

_____

_____

_____

CHOPPED _____
VIBEY WORD
SALAD FOR A CROWD

① Unearth your largest bowl and pour a big spoonful or two of _____
YOUR FAVORITE DRESSING
over the bottom.

② Call a general assembly of non-greens salad components: up to 2 cups each of

_____ , _____ ,
PROTEIN   CRUNCHY RAW THINGS

_____ , _____ ,
BRINY THINGS   JUICY THINGS

and _____ , plus up to 1 cup _____ ,
TENDER THINGS   CHEWY DRIED THINGS

in any combination that makes your heart sing. Chop them all into small, uniform pieces

and toss them into the bowl. Slosh them around in the dressing, then leave them alone to

do team-building activities.

③ Chop a head of _____ and a head's worth of
CRISPY GREENS

_____ . Fold them both in with the rest and add up to 2 cups
DARK LEAFY GREENS

crumbled or grated _____ cheese.
TYPE OF CHEESE

④ Finish it off with _____ or _____ ,
FRESH HERBS   SOMETHING TO SCATTER ON TOP

then serve.

HINTS AND WINKS

ANYTHING-GOES VINAIGRETTE

VIBEY WORD
- Waldorf
- Cobb
- Southwestern
- summertime
- kitchen sink

YOUR FAVORITE DRESSING
- olive oil and lemon juice
- blue cheese
- green goddess
- carrot-ginger
- **Anything-Goes Vinaigrette**

PROTEIN
- shredded cooked chicken
- canned tuna
- hard-boiled egg
- sliced salami
- canned or cooked chickpeas

CRUNCHY RAW THINGS
- celery
- Granny Smith apple
- cucumber
- radishes
- snow peas
- shaved fennel

BRINY THINGS
- capers
- pitted olives
- cornichons
- pepperoncini
- marinated artichoke hearts

JUICY THINGS
- cherry tomatoes
- grapes
- blueberries
- citrus segments

TENDER THINGS
- corn kernels
- diced avocado
- cooked waxy potatoes
- peas
- butterfly kisses

CHEWY DRIED THINGS
- golden or dark raisins
- dried cranberries or apricots
- sun-dried tomatoes

CRISPY GREENS
- iceberg or romaine lettuce
- radicchio
- Brussels sprouts
- red or green cabbage

DARK LEAFY GREENS
- kale
- Swiss chard
- spinach

TYPE OF CHEESE
- cheddar
- provolone
- feta

FRESH HERBS
- cilantro
- parsley
- mint
- basil

SOMETHING TO SCATTER ON TOP
- everything bagel seasoning
- sliced scallions
- bacon bits
- toasted pepitas

You'll need acid and fat in a roughly 1:3 ratio (but there's wiggle room if you want something a little more bracing or mild). Pick the **acid** first: balsamic, cider, wine, champagne, sherry, or rice vinegar will keep your salad perky. As for **fat,** a good olive oil will contribute its own flavor, while a neutral oil like grapeseed or canola won't compete. Friends like toasted sesame oil, walnut oil, and even bacon fat can be great, but don't use too much or it'll yell over everything else. The sky's the limit for **seasoning:** salt is mandatory, while spices; fish sauce or soy sauce; and minced fresh herbs, alliums, ginger, and capers are all fun and advisable. Combine everything in a bowl or a lidded jar and whisk or shake to incorporate.

NOTES TO YOUR FUTURE SELF

CHOPPED _____
VIBEY WORD
SALAD FOR A CROWD

① Unearth your largest bowl and pour a big spoonful or two of _____
YOUR FAVORITE DRESSING

over the bottom.

② Call a general assembly of non-greens salad components: up to 2 cups each of

_____ , _____ ,
PROTEIN   CRUNCHY RAW THINGS

_____ , _____ ,
BRINY THINGS   JUICY THINGS

and _____ , plus up to 1 cup _____ ,
TENDER THINGS   CHEWY DRIED THINGS

in any combination that makes your heart sing. Chop them all into small, uniform pieces

and toss them into the bowl. Slosh them around in the dressing, then leave them alone to

do team-building activities.

③ Chop a head of _____ and a head's worth of
CRISPY GREENS

_____ . Fold them both in with the rest and add up to 2 cups
DARK LEAFY GREENS

crumbled or grated _____ cheese.
TYPE OF CHEESE

④ Finish it off with _____ or _____ ,
FRESH HERBS   SOMETHING TO SCATTER ON TOP

then serve.

HINTS AND WINKS

VIBEY WORD
- Waldorf
- Cobb
- Southwestern
- summertime
- kitchen sink

YOUR FAVORITE DRESSING
- olive oil and lemon juice
- blue cheese
- green goddess
- carrot-ginger
- **Anything-Goes Vinaigrette**

PROTEIN
- shredded cooked chicken
- canned tuna
- hard-boiled egg
- sliced salami
- canned or cooked chickpeas

CRUNCHY RAW THINGS
- celery
- Granny Smith apple
- cucumber
- radishes
- snow peas
- shaved fennel

BRINY THINGS
- capers
- pitted olives
- cornichons
- pepperoncini
- marinated artichoke hearts

JUICY THINGS
- cherry tomatoes
- grapes
- blueberries
- citrus segments

TENDER THINGS
- corn kernels
- diced avocado
- cooked waxy potatoes
- peas
- butterfly kisses

CHEWY DRIED THINGS
- golden or dark raisins
- dried cranberries or apricots
- sun-dried tomatoes

CRISPY GREENS
- iceberg or romaine lettuce
- radicchio
- Brussels sprouts
- red or green cabbage

DARK LEAFY GREENS
- kale
- Swiss chard
- spinach

TYPE OF CHEESE
- cheddar
- provolone
- feta

FRESH HERBS
- cilantro
- parsley
- mint
- basil

SOMETHING TO SCATTER ON TOP
- everything bagel seasoning
- sliced scallions
- bacon bits
- toasted pepitas

ANYTHING-GOES VINAIGRETTE

You'll need acid and fat in a roughly 1:3 ratio (but there's wiggle room if you want something a little more bracing or mild). Pick the **acid** first: balsamic, cider, wine, champagne, sherry, or rice vinegar will keep your salad perky. As for **fat,** a good olive oil will contribute its own flavor, while a neutral oil like grapeseed or canola won't compete. Friends like toasted sesame oil, walnut oil, and even bacon fat can be great, but don't use too much or it'll yell over everything else. The sky's the limit for **seasoning:** salt is mandatory, while spices; fish sauce or soy sauce; and minced fresh herbs, alliums, ginger, and capers are all fun and advisable. Combine everything in a bowl or a lidded jar and whisk or shake to incorporate.

NOTES TO YOUR FUTURE SELF

_____

_____

_____

_____

_____

CHOPPED _____
VIBEY WORD
SALAD FOR A CROWD

① Unearth your largest bowl and pour a big spoonful or two of _____
YOUR FAVORITE DRESSING

over the bottom.

② Call a general assembly of non-greens salad components: up to 2 cups each of

_____ , _____ ,
PROTEIN   CRUNCHY RAW THINGS

_____ , _____ ,
BRINY THINGS   JUICY THINGS

and _____ , plus up to 1 cup _____ ,
TENDER THINGS   CHEWY DRIED THINGS

in any combination that makes your heart sing. Chop them all into small, uniform pieces

and toss them into the bowl. Slosh them around in the dressing, then leave them alone to

do team-building activities.

③ Chop a head of _____ and a head's worth of
CRISPY GREENS

_____ . Fold them both in with the rest and add up to 2 cups
DARK LEAFY GREENS

crumbled or grated _____ cheese.
TYPE OF CHEESE

④ Finish it off with _____ or _____ ,
FRESH HERBS   SOMETHING TO SCATTER ON TOP

then serve.

HINTS AND WINKS

VIBEY WORD
- Waldorf
- Cobb
- Southwestern
- summertime
- kitchen sink

YOUR FAVORITE DRESSING
- olive oil and lemon juice
- blue cheese
- green goddess
- carrot-ginger
- **Anything-Goes Vinaigrette**

PROTEIN
- shredded cooked chicken
- canned tuna
- hard-boiled egg
- sliced salami
- canned or cooked chickpeas

CRUNCHY RAW THINGS
- celery
- Granny Smith apple
- cucumber
- radishes
- snow peas
- shaved fennel

BRINY THINGS
- capers
- pitted olives
- cornichons
- pepperoncini
- marinated artichoke hearts

JUICY THINGS
- cherry tomatoes
- grapes
- blueberries
- citrus segments

TENDER THINGS
- corn kernels
- diced avocado
- cooked waxy potatoes
- peas
- butterfly kisses

CHEWY DRIED THINGS
- golden or dark raisins
- dried cranberries or apricots
- sun-dried tomatoes

CRISPY GREENS
- iceberg or romaine lettuce
- radicchio
- Brussels sprouts
- red or green cabbage

DARK LEAFY GREENS
- kale
- Swiss chard
- spinach

TYPE OF CHEESE
- cheddar
- provolone
- feta

FRESH HERBS
- cilantro
- parsley
- mint
- basil

SOMETHING TO SCATTER ON TOP
- everything bagel seasoning
- sliced scallions
- bacon bits
- toasted pepitas

ANYTHING-GOES VINAIGRETTE

You'll need acid and fat in a roughly 1:3 ratio (but there's wiggle room if you want something a little more bracing or mild). Pick the **acid** first: balsamic, cider, wine, champagne, sherry, or rice vinegar will keep your salad perky. As for **fat,** a good olive oil will contribute its own flavor, while a neutral oil like grapeseed or canola won't compete. Friends like toasted sesame oil, walnut oil, and even bacon fat can be great, but don't use too much or it'll yell over everything else. The sky's the limit for **seasoning:** salt is mandatory, while spices; fish sauce or soy sauce; and minced fresh herbs, alliums, ginger, and capers are all fun and advisable. Combine everything in a bowl or a lidded jar and whisk or shake to incorporate.

NOTES TO YOUR FUTURE SELF

_____

_____

_____

_____

_____

EGGS BAKED IN

_____

SCRUMPTIOUS CUSHY BED

_____

① Preheat the oven to 375°F. Lightly grease _____ with
                                            OVENPROOF VESSEL(S)

_____ .
COOKING FAT

② Figure 1 or 2 eggs per serving. For every serving, put a little less than a cup of

_____ in the dish. You can sneak a slice of
SCRUMPTIOUS CUSHY BED

_____ beneath this mess and even top it off with some
BREAD PRODUCT

_____ , as long as the eggs have somewhere to make a soft
WOW FACTOR

landing while they bake.

③ With the back of your spoon, make little divots and crack an egg inside each,

followed by a pinch each of salt and pepper. If you're feeling lush, top with dribs and

drabs of _____ , a sprinkle of _____ ,
          SOMETHING RICH   SOMETHING THAT'LL GET CRISPY

and/or a shower of _____ .
                    GRATED HARD CHEESE

④ Bake until the egg whites are opaque and the yolks are still a little jiggly, 8 to 10 minutes.

Kick up your heels and eat it right away, or top it with _____ .
                                                          A LI'L SOMETHING EXTRA

HINTS AND WINKS

SCRUMPTIOUS CUSHY BED
- mashed potatoes
- caramelized onions
- sautéed or creamed greens
- ratatouille
- cooked lentils or beans
- cooked grits
- **Really Easy Tomato Sauce**

OVENPROOF VESSEL(S)
- individual ramekins (one per serving)
- cast-iron skillet
- casserole dish

COOKING FAT
- olive oil
- butter
- pork or bacon fat

BREAD PRODUCT
- English muffin
- challah
- brioche
- whole-grain bread

WOW FACTOR
- sliced ham
- goat cheese
- ricotta
- Brie
- Greek yogurt seasoned with spices

SOMETHING RICH
- heavy cream
- olive oil
- gold leaf

SOMETHING THAT'LL GET CRISPY
- panko
- bread crumbs

GRATED HARD CHEESE
- Parmesan or pecorino
- cheddar

A LI'L SOMETHING EXTRA
- hollandaise
- chopped fresh herbs
- more of your Wow Factor from earlier

WHIP IT UP

REALLY EASY TOMATO SAUCE

Heat **3 tablespoons oil or butter** in a saucepan. Add a handful of **chopped onion** and a pinch of **salt** and cook, stirring, for a few minutes, until the onion is soft. Add some **minced garlic, paprika, red pepper flakes,** and/or **tomato paste** and cook until the tomato paste is toasty and it's all smelling good. Dump in a **28-ounce can of crushed tomatoes** and bring to a simmer. Cook until the bubbles start to slow down. (This makes enough for 4 servings but can easily be doubled or tripled.)

NOTES TO YOUR FUTURE SELF

_____

_____

_____

_____

_____

EGGS BAKED IN

_____

SCRUMPTIOUS CUSHY BED

① Preheat the oven to 375°F. Lightly grease _____ with
OVENPROOF VESSEL(S)

_____ .
COOKING FAT

② Figure 1 or 2 eggs per serving. For every serving, put a little less than a cup of

_____ in the dish. You can sneak a slice of
SCRUMPTIOUS CUSHY BED

_____ beneath this mess and even top it off with some
BREAD PRODUCT

_____ , as long as the eggs have somewhere to make a soft
WOW FACTOR

landing while they bake.

③ With the back of your spoon, make little divots and crack an egg inside each,

followed by a pinch each of salt and pepper. If you're feeling lush, top with dribs and

drabs of _____ , a sprinkle of _____ ,
SOMETHING RICH   SOMETHING THAT'LL GET CRISPY

and/or a shower of _____ .
GRATED HARD CHEESE

④ Bake until the egg whites are opaque and the yolks are still a little jiggly, 8 to 10 minutes.

Kick up your heels and eat it right away, or top it with _____ .
A LI'L SOMETHING EXTRA

HINTS AND WINKS

SCRUMPTIOUS CUSHY BED
- mashed potatoes
- caramelized onions
- sautéed or creamed greens
- ratatouille
- cooked lentils or beans
- cooked grits
- **Really Easy Tomato Sauce**

OVENPROOF VESSEL(S)
- individual ramekins (one per serving)
- cast-iron skillet
- casserole dish

COOKING FAT
- olive oil
- butter
- pork or bacon fat

BREAD PRODUCT
- English muffin
- challah
- brioche
- whole-grain bread

WOW FACTOR
- sliced ham
- goat cheese
- ricotta
- Brie
- Greek yogurt seasoned with spices

SOMETHING RICH
- heavy cream
- olive oil
- gold leaf

SOMETHING THAT'LL GET CRISPY
- panko
- bread crumbs

GRATED HARD CHEESE
- Parmesan or pecorino
- cheddar

A LI'L SOMETHING EXTRA
- hollandaise
- chopped fresh herbs
- more of your Wow Factor from earlier

REALLY EASY TOMATO SAUCE

Heat **3 tablespoons oil or butter** in a saucepan. Add a handful of **chopped onion** and a pinch of **salt** and cook, stirring, for a few minutes, until the onion is soft. Add some **minced garlic, paprika, red pepper flakes,** and/or **tomato paste** and cook until the tomato paste is toasty and it's all smelling good. Dump in a **28-ounce can of crushed tomatoes** and bring to a simmer. Cook until the bubbles start to slow down. (This makes enough for 4 servings but can easily be doubled or tripled.)

NOTES TO YOUR FUTURE SELF

_____

_____

_____

_____

_____

EGGS BAKED IN

_____

SCRUMPTIOUS CUSHY BED

① Preheat the oven to 375°F. Lightly grease _____ with
OVENPROOF VESSEL(S)

_____ .
COOKING FAT

② Figure 1 or 2 eggs per serving. For every serving, put a little less than a cup of

_____ in the dish. You can sneak a slice of
SCRUMPTIOUS CUSHY BED

_____ beneath this mess and even top it off with some
BREAD PRODUCT

_____ , as long as the eggs have somewhere to make a soft
WOW FACTOR

landing while they bake.

③ With the back of your spoon, make little divots and crack an egg inside each,

followed by a pinch each of salt and pepper. If you're feeling lush, top with dribs and

drabs of _____ , a sprinkle of _____ ,
SOMETHING RICH   SOMETHING THAT'LL GET CRISPY

and/or a shower of _____ .
GRATED HARD CHEESE

④ Bake until the egg whites are opaque and the yolks are still a little jiggly, 8 to 10 minutes.

Kick up your heels and eat it right away, or top it with _____ .
A LI'L SOMETHING EXTRA

HINTS AND WINKS

SCRUMPTIOUS CUSHY BED
- mashed potatoes
- caramelized onions
- sautéed or creamed greens
- ratatouille
- cooked lentils or beans
- cooked grits
- **Really Easy Tomato Sauce**

OVENPROOF VESSEL(S)
- individual ramekins (one per serving)
- cast-iron skillet
- casserole dish

COOKING FAT
- olive oil
- butter
- pork or bacon fat

BREAD PRODUCT
- English muffin
- challah
- brioche
- whole-grain bread

WOW FACTOR
- sliced ham
- goat cheese
- ricotta
- Brie
- Greek yogurt seasoned with spices

SOMETHING RICH
- heavy cream
- olive oil
- gold leaf

SOMETHING THAT'LL GET CRISPY
- panko
- bread crumbs

GRATED HARD CHEESE
- Parmesan or pecorino
- cheddar

A LI'L SOMETHING EXTRA
- hollandaise
- chopped fresh herbs
- more of your Wow Factor from earlier

REALLY EASY TOMATO SAUCE

Heat **3 tablespoons oil or butter** in a saucepan. Add a handful of **chopped onion** and a pinch of **salt** and cook, stirring, for a few minutes, until the onion is soft. Add some **minced garlic, paprika, red pepper flakes,** and/or **tomato paste** and cook until the tomato paste is toasty and it's all smelling good. Dump in a **28-ounce can of crushed tomatoes** and bring to a simmer. Cook until the bubbles start to slow down. (This makes enough for 4 servings but can easily be doubled or tripled.)

NOTES TO YOUR FUTURE SELF

_____

_____

_____

_____

_____

WORDS THAT'LL MAKE YOU FEEL WARM & FUZZY
NOODLE SOUP

① Fill a large stockpot with a couple quarts of _____ and salt
                                                 COOKING LIQUID

liberally. Toss in some _____ and, if you've got them, some
                          AROMATICS

_____ . Bring to a lively simmer, then let it putter away for about
EXCLAMATION POINTS

a half hour to let the flavors coalesce.

② Strain the stock. For something brothier and more straightforward, return it to the pot now.

You can also heat a few tablespoons of olive oil and toast an equal amount of

_____ paste until it's fragrant, then swish in the stock, or add up
        TASTY PASTE

to 2 cups of _____ to make whatever's in your pot a teeny bit
              SOMETHING LUSCIOUS

more velvety and bisque-esque.

③ Bring it all to a boil and add a few cups of chopped _____ .
                                                        STURDY VEGETABLES

Cook until they're tender, then tip in about ½ pound of _____
                                                         NOODLES

and cook them for a few minutes, until they're just shy of al dente.

④ Turn off the heat and swirl in up to 3 cups of _____ , plus a
                                                  PROTEIN

limitless supply of _____ . If you've got a couple cups, give or
                     VEG THAT'LL BLEND RIGHT IN

take, of _____ , dunk those in, too.
          VEG THAT'LL STAY LIVELY

⑤ Taste the soup and splash in some _____ , if you want;
                                      FINAL TOUCH

don't overthink this. Dig out the bowl that most resembles a Jacuzzi hot tub and fill 'er

up. Top with a fistful of _____ . Eat it while it's hot!
                           FANCIFUL GARNISH

HINTS AND WINKS

WORDS THAT'LL MAKE YOU FEEL WARM & FUZZY
- soul-soothing
- creamy
- hearty
- spicy

COOKING LIQUID
- water
- stock (chicken, vegetable, or mushroom)

AROMATICS
- diced onions
- bay leaves
- crushed garlic
- minced ginger or lemongrass
- fresh or dried herbs
- star anise pods
- cinnamon sticks
- whole black peppercorns

EXCLAMATION POINTS
- bones or carcasses from cooked meat or poultry
- shrimp heads or shells
- dashi
- dried mushrooms
- red or white wine
- Parmesan rinds

TASTY PASTE
- curry
- chili
- tomato

SOMETHING LUSCIOUS
- coconut milk
- heavy cream
- canned tomato purée

STURDY VEGETABLES
- carrots or parsnips
- celery stalks
- mushrooms
- sweet potatoes

NOODLES
- fusilli
- egg noodles
- wonton wrappers
- vermicelli

PROTEIN
- shredded cooked chicken or turkey
- thinly sliced raw beef
- braised short ribs
- cooked meatballs
- cooked beans or chickpeas

VEG THAT'LL BLEND RIGHT IN
- kale
- spinach
- bok choy
- seaweed
- endive or escarole
- cabbage

VEG THAT'LL STAY LIVELY
- snow peas
- corn
- cherry tomatoes
- broccoli florets

FINAL TOUCH
- miso slurry
- fish sauce
- soy sauce
- lemon or lime juice
- yuzu kosho
- mirin
- beaten raw eggs

FANCIFUL GARNISH
- fried shallots
- mung bean sprouts
- cilantro or parsley
- sliced scallions
- kimchi

TIP
STOCK ON THE SPOT

If you don't have quarts of homemade stock lying around, you can make one with raw ingredients that you'll be adding to the soup—chicken, mushrooms, and other vegetables perform famously. Add them to a pot of water with all your aromatics in step 1, then pull them out when they're finished cooking and reintroduce them in step 4.

NOTES TO YOUR FUTURE SELF

_____

_____

_____

_____

WORDS THAT'LL MAKE YOU FEEL WARM & FUZZY

NOODLE SOUP

① Fill a large stockpot with a couple quarts of _____ and salt
                                                COOKING LIQUID

liberally. Toss in some _____ and, if you've got them, some
                         AROMATICS

_____ . Bring to a lively simmer, then let it putter away for about
EXCLAMATION POINTS

a half hour to let the flavors coalesce.

② Strain the stock. For something brothier and more straightforward, return it to the pot now.

You can also heat a few tablespoons of olive oil and toast an equal amount of

_____ paste until it's fragrant, then swish in the stock, or add up
TASTY PASTE

to 2 cups of _____ to make whatever's in your pot a teeny bit
              SOMETHING LUSCIOUS

more velvety and bisque-esque.

③ Bring it all to a boil and add a few cups of chopped _____ .
                                                        STURDY VEGETABLES

Cook until they're tender, then tip in about ½ pound of _____
                                                         NOODLES

and cook them for a few minutes, until they're just shy of al dente.

④ Turn off the heat and swirl in up to 3 cups of _____ , plus a
                                                  PROTEIN

limitless supply of _____ . If you've got a couple cups, give or
                     VEG THAT'LL BLEND RIGHT IN

take, of _____ , dunk those in, too.
          VEG THAT'LL STAY LIVELY

⑤ Taste the soup and splash in some _____ , if you want;
                                      FINAL TOUCH

don't overthink this. Dig out the bowl that most resembles a Jacuzzi hot tub and fill 'er

up. Top with a fistful of _____ . Eat it while it's hot!
                           FANCIFUL GARNISH

HINTS AND WINKS

WORDS THAT'LL MAKE YOU FEEL WARM & FUZZY
- soul-soothing
- creamy
- hearty
- spicy

COOKING LIQUID
- water
- stock (chicken, vegetable, or mushroom)

AROMATICS
- diced onions
- bay leaves
- crushed garlic
- minced ginger or lemongrass
- fresh or dried herbs
- star anise pods
- cinnamon sticks
- whole black peppercorns

EXCLAMATION POINTS
- bones or carcasses from cooked meat or poultry
- shrimp heads or shells
- dashi
- dried mushrooms
- red or white wine
- Parmesan rinds

TASTY PASTE
- curry
- chili
- tomato

SOMETHING LUSCIOUS
- coconut milk
- heavy cream
- canned tomato purée

STURDY VEGETABLES
- carrots or parsnips
- celery stalks
- mushrooms
- sweet potatoes

NOODLES
- fusilli
- egg noodles
- wonton wrappers
- vermicelli

PROTEIN
- shredded cooked chicken or turkey
- thinly sliced raw beef
- braised short ribs
- cooked meatballs
- cooked beans or chickpeas

VEG THAT'LL BLEND RIGHT IN
- kale
- spinach
- bok choy
- seaweed
- endive or escarole
- cabbage

VEG THAT'LL STAY LIVELY
- snow peas
- corn
- cherry tomatoes
- broccoli florets

FINAL TOUCH
- miso slurry
- fish sauce
- soy sauce
- lemon or lime juice
- yuzu kosho
- mirin
- beaten raw eggs

FANCIFUL GARNISH
- fried shallots
- mung bean sprouts
- cilantro or parsley
- sliced scallions
- kimchi

TIP

STOCK ON THE SPOT

If you don't have quarts of homemade stock lying around, you can make one with raw ingredients that you'll be adding to the soup—chicken, mushrooms, and other vegetables perform famously. Add them to a pot of water with all your aromatics in step 1, then pull them out when they're finished cooking and reintroduce them in step 4.

NOTES TO YOUR FUTURE SELF

_____

_____

_____

_____

WORDS THAT'LL MAKE YOU FEEL WARM & FUZZY

NOODLE SOUP

① Fill a large stockpot with a couple quarts of _____ and salt
COOKING LIQUID

liberally. Toss in some _____ and, if you've got them, some
AROMATICS

_____ . Bring to a lively simmer, then let it putter away for about
EXCLAMATION POINTS

a half hour to let the flavors coalesce.

② Strain the stock. For something brothier and more straightforward, return it to the pot now.

You can also heat a few tablespoons of olive oil and toast an equal amount of

_____ paste until it's fragrant, then swish in the stock, or add up
TASTY PASTE

to 2 cups of _____ to make whatever's in your pot a teeny bit
SOMETHING LUSCIOUS

more velvety and bisque-esque.

③ Bring it all to a boil and add a few cups of chopped _____ .
STURDY VEGETABLES

Cook until they're tender, then tip in about ½ pound of _____
NOODLES

and cook them for a few minutes, until they're just shy of al dente.

④ Turn off the heat and swirl in up to 3 cups of _____ , plus a
PROTEIN

limitless supply of _____ . If you've got a couple cups, give or
VEG THAT'LL BLEND RIGHT IN

take, of _____ , dunk those in, too.
VEG THAT'LL STAY LIVELY

⑤ Taste the soup and splash in some _____ , if you want;
FINAL TOUCH

don't overthink this. Dig out the bowl that most resembles a Jacuzzi hot tub and fill 'er

up. Top with a fistful of _____ . Eat it while it's hot!
FANCIFUL GARNISH

HINTS AND WINKS

WORDS THAT'LL MAKE YOU FEEL WARM & FUZZY
- soul-soothing
- creamy
- hearty
- spicy

COOKING LIQUID
- water
- stock (chicken, vegetable, or mushroom)

AROMATICS
- diced onions
- bay leaves
- crushed garlic
- minced ginger or lemongrass
- fresh or dried herbs
- star anise pods
- cinnamon sticks
- whole black peppercorns

EXCLAMATION POINTS
- bones or carcasses from cooked meat or poultry
- shrimp heads or shells
- dashi
- dried mushrooms
- red or white wine
- Parmesan rinds

TASTY PASTE
- curry
- chili
- tomato

SOMETHING LUSCIOUS
- coconut milk
- heavy cream
- canned tomato purée

STURDY VEGETABLES
- carrots or parsnips
- celery stalks
- mushrooms
- sweet potatoes

NOODLES
- fusilli
- egg noodles
- wonton wrappers
- vermicelli

PROTEIN
- shredded cooked chicken or turkey
- thinly sliced raw beef
- braised short ribs
- cooked meatballs
- cooked beans or chickpeas

VEG THAT'LL BLEND RIGHT IN
- kale
- spinach
- bok choy
- seaweed
- endive or escarole
- cabbage

VEG THAT'LL STAY LIVELY
- snow peas
- corn
- cherry tomatoes
- broccoli florets

FINAL TOUCH
- miso slurry
- fish sauce
- soy sauce
- lemon or lime juice
- yuzu kosho
- mirin
- beaten raw eggs

FANCIFUL GARNISH
- fried shallots
- mung bean sprouts
- cilantro or parsley
- sliced scallions
- kimchi

NOTES TO YOUR FUTURE SELF

_____

_____

_____

_____

_____ BURGERS WITH
PROTEIN

_____
BELLS & WHISTLES

① Start with 2 pounds (give or take) raw _____ (which should
PROTEIN

be enough for 8 burgers). If it isn't already ground, cut it down into small, evenly sized

pieces and stick it in the fridge for an hour. If it's ground, skip ahead to step 3!

(And if your protein is a veggie burger, fast-forward to step 4.)

② Transfer the chilled meat to your food processor. Pulse until the meat is well chopped but

not pasty.

③ Stick the meat in a large bowl and leave it alone, or add some minced or grated

_____ , a two-finger pinch of _____ , chopped
ALLIUMS   SPICES

_____ , and an enthusiastic shake of _____
FRESH HERBS   TYPE OF SAUCE

sauce. If the meat's on the leaner side, add _____ to keep it
SOMETHING RICH & MELTY

tender. If you're feeling fancy, add some crumbled _____ cheese
CRUMBLY CHEESE

and maybe a couple tablespoons of _____ .
SOMETHING ZINGY

④ Coax everything together with a spatula—don't overwork it—then coyly shape the meat

into patties the size of your palm, to make 8 of them. Make a dimple in the center of each

with the pad of your thumb and rain salt and pepper over both sides.

⑤ Set a large, heavy skillet over medium heat and get it very hot, then add the patties

(don't crowd them) and cook them, undisturbed, for 3 to 5 minutes per side—this'll leave

a center that's still juicy and a burger that feels springy, not soft. Once that's done, top

your patties with a slice of _____ cheese and let them sit in
ANY OTHER CHEESE

quiet repose while you toast some _____ .
FANCY BUNS

⑥ Lavish the inside of each bun with _____ and add a burger,
YOUR FAVORITE CONDIMENTS

a dainty amount of _____ , and _____ .
ROUGHAGE   BELLS & WHISTLES

HINTS AND WINKS

PROTEIN
- beef
- turkey
- lamb
- shrimp
- salmon
- **Veggie Burgers**

BELLS & WHISTLES
- sliced avocado
- cooked bacon slices
- fried eggs
- onion rings
- sautéed mushrooms
- potato chips

ALLIUMS
- white, red, or yellow onion
- garlic

SPICES
- red pepper flakes
- ground cumin
- smoked paprika
- fennel seeds

FRESH HERBS
- tarragon
- mint
- cilantro
- parsley

TYPE OF SAUCE
- barbecue
- Worcestershire
- fish
- hot

SOMETHING RICH & MELTY
- an egg
- grated butter
- mayonnaise

CRUMBLY CHEESE
- feta
- blue
- goat
- cotija

SOMETHING ZINGY
- minced lemongrass or ginger
- minced chile
- capers

ANY OTHER CHEESE
- American
- cheddar
- Swiss or Gruyère
- pepper Jack
- Brie

FANCY BUNS
- challah or brioche
- pretzel or potato roll
- ciabatta
- sesame seed bun

YOUR FAVORITE CONDIMENTS
- mayonnaise (flavored with sriracha, canned chipotles, or fresh herbs)
- pesto
- hoisin sauce
- peanut butter (yes!)

ROUGHAGE
- sliced tomato or cucumber
- iceberg or romaine lettuce
- arugula
- watercress

VEGGIE BURGERS

Combine about **2 cups lentils or beans** (cooked or canned) with **1 or 2 eggs** (real or flax), **½ cup bread crumbs,** and your favorite **spices, herbs, or condiments**. If you've got **leftover cooked rice or grains,** you can throw in up to ½ cup; a cup or so of **grated or finely chopped raw vegetables** will be right at home, too. Pulse in a food processor until everything is incorporated and coarsely chopped. Then start at step 4.

NOTES TO YOUR FUTURE SELF

_____

_____

_____

_____

_____

_____ BURGERS WITH
PROTEIN

_____
BELLS & WHISTLES

① Start with 2 pounds (give or take) raw _____ (which should
PROTEIN

be enough for 8 burgers). If it isn't already ground, cut it down into small, evenly sized

pieces and stick it in the fridge for an hour. If it's ground, skip ahead to step 3!

(And if your protein is a veggie burger, fast-forward to step 4.)

② Transfer the chilled meat to your food processor. Pulse until the meat is well chopped but

not pasty.

③ Stick the meat in a large bowl and leave it alone, or add some minced or grated

_____ , a two-finger pinch of _____ , chopped
ALLIUMS   SPICES

_____ , and an enthusiastic shake of _____
FRESH HERBS   TYPE OF SAUCE

sauce. If the meat's on the leaner side, add _____ to keep it
SOMETHING RICH & MELTY

tender. If you're feeling fancy, add some crumbled _____ cheese
CRUMBLY CHEESE

and maybe a couple tablespoons of _____ .
SOMETHING ZINGY

④ Coax everything together with a spatula—don't overwork it—then coyly shape the meat

into patties the size of your palm, to make 8 of them. Make a dimple in the center of each

with the pad of your thumb and rain salt and pepper over both sides.

⑤ Set a large, heavy skillet over medium heat and get it very hot, then add the patties

(don't crowd them) and cook them, undisturbed, for 3 to 5 minutes per side—this'll leave

a center that's still juicy and a burger that feels springy, not soft. Once that's done, top

your patties with a slice of _____ cheese and let them sit in
ANY OTHER CHEESE

quiet repose while you toast some _____ .
FANCY BUNS

⑥ Lavish the inside of each bun with _____ and add a burger,
YOUR FAVORITE CONDIMENTS

a dainty amount of _____ , and _____ .
ROUGHAGE   BELLS & WHISTLES

HINTS AND WINKS

PROTEIN
- beef
- turkey
- lamb
- shrimp
- salmon
- **Veggie Burgers**

BELLS & WHISTLES
- sliced avocado
- cooked bacon slices
- fried eggs
- onion rings
- sautéed mushrooms
- potato chips

ALLIUMS
- white, red, or yellow onion
- garlic

SPICES
- red pepper flakes
- ground cumin
- smoked paprika
- fennel seeds

FRESH HERBS
- tarragon
- mint
- cilantro
- parsley

TYPE OF SAUCE
- barbecue
- Worcestershire
- fish
- hot

SOMETHING RICH & MELTY
- an egg
- grated butter
- mayonnaise

CRUMBLY CHEESE
- feta
- blue
- goat
- cotija

SOMETHING ZINGY
- minced lemongrass or ginger
- minced chile
- capers

ANY OTHER CHEESE
- American
- cheddar
- Swiss or Gruyère
- pepper Jack
- Brie

FANCY BUNS
- challah or brioche
- pretzel or potato roll
- ciabatta
- sesame seed bun

YOUR FAVORITE CONDIMENTS
- mayonnaise (flavored with sriracha, canned chipotles, or fresh herbs)
- pesto
- hoisin sauce
- peanut butter (yes!)

ROUGHAGE
- sliced tomato or cucumber
- iceberg or romaine lettuce
- arugula
- watercress

VEGGIE BURGERS

Combine about **2 cups lentils or beans** (cooked or canned) with **1 or 2 eggs** (real or flax), **½ cup bread crumbs,** and your favorite **spices, herbs, or condiments**. If you've got **leftover cooked rice or grains,** you can throw in up to ½ cup; a cup or so of **grated or finely chopped raw vegetables** will be right at home, too. Pulse in a food processor until everything is incorporated and coarsely chopped. Then start at step 4.

NOTES TO YOUR FUTURE SELF

_____

_____

_____

_____

BURGERS WITH

_____
PROTEIN

_____
BELLS & WHISTLES

① Start with 2 pounds (give or take) raw _____ (which should
PROTEIN

be enough for 8 burgers). If it isn't already ground, cut it down into small, evenly sized

pieces and stick it in the fridge for an hour. If it's ground, skip ahead to step 3!

(And if your protein is a veggie burger, fast-forward to step 4.)

② Transfer the chilled meat to your food processor. Pulse until the meat is well chopped but

not pasty.

③ Stick the meat in a large bowl and leave it alone, or add some minced or grated

_____ , a two-finger pinch of _____ , chopped
ALLIUMS   SPICES

_____ , and an enthusiastic shake of _____
FRESH HERBS   TYPE OF SAUCE

sauce. If the meat's on the leaner side, add _____ to keep it
SOMETHING RICH & MELTY

tender. If you're feeling fancy, add some crumbled _____ cheese
CRUMBLY CHEESE

and maybe a couple tablespoons of _____ .
SOMETHING ZINGY

④ Coax everything together with a spatula—don't overwork it—then coyly shape the meat

into patties the size of your palm, to make 8 of them. Make a dimple in the center of each

with the pad of your thumb and rain salt and pepper over both sides.

⑤ Set a large, heavy skillet over medium heat and get it very hot, then add the patties

(don't crowd them) and cook them, undisturbed, for 3 to 5 minutes per side—this'll leave

a center that's still juicy and a burger that feels springy, not soft. Once that's done, top

your patties with a slice of _____ cheese and let them sit in
ANY OTHER CHEESE

quiet repose while you toast some _____ .
FANCY BUNS

⑥ Lavish the inside of each bun with _____ and add a burger,
YOUR FAVORITE CONDIMENTS

a dainty amount of _____ , and _____ .
ROUGHAGE   BELLS & WHISTLES

HINTS AND WINKS

PROTEIN
- beef
- turkey
- lamb
- shrimp
- salmon
- **Veggie Burgers**

BELLS & WHISTLES
- sliced avocado
- cooked bacon slices
- fried eggs
- onion rings
- sautéed mushrooms
- potato chips

ALLIUMS
- white, red, or yellow onion
- garlic

SPICES
- red pepper flakes
- ground cumin
- smoked paprika
- fennel seeds

FRESH HERBS
- tarragon
- mint
- cilantro
- parsley

TYPE OF SAUCE
- barbecue
- Worcestershire
- fish
- hot

SOMETHING RICH & MELTY
- an egg
- grated butter
- mayonnaise

CRUMBLY CHEESE
- feta
- blue
- goat
- cotija

SOMETHING ZINGY
- minced lemongrass or ginger
- minced chile
- capers

ANY OTHER CHEESE
- American
- cheddar
- Swiss or Gruyère
- pepper Jack
- Brie

FANCY BUNS
- challah or brioche
- pretzel or potato roll
- ciabatta
- sesame seed bun

YOUR FAVORITE CONDIMENTS
- mayonnaise (flavored with sriracha, canned chipotles, or fresh herbs)
- pesto
- hoisin sauce
- peanut butter (yes!)

ROUGHAGE
- sliced tomato or cucumber
- iceberg or romaine lettuce
- arugula
- watercress

VEGGIE BURGERS

Combine about **2 cups lentils or beans** (cooked or canned) with **1 or 2 eggs** (real or flax), **½ cup bread crumbs,** and your favorite **spices, herbs, or condiments**. If you've got **leftover cooked rice or grains,** you can throw in up to ½ cup; a cup or so of **grated or finely chopped raw vegetables** will be right at home, too. Pulse in a food processor until everything is incorporated and coarsely chopped. Then start at step 4.

NOTES TO YOUR FUTURE SELF

_____

_____

_____

_____

FRIED _____ WITH
RICE OR GRAINS

&
_____ & _____
VEG   PROTEIN

① Take a second to gather your thoughts and ingredients. This dish cooks quickly, so you'll want to make sure everything's chopped, prepped, and ready to rock and roll when you need it.

② Drag out a big skillet or wok and heat it over high heat for a minute, then swirl in a couple tablespoons of _____ . When the oil is shimmery-shiny, reduce
HIGH-SMOKE-POINT FAT
the heat to medium and add about 1 cup diced _____ and some
ALLIUMS
chopped/crushed _____ .
AROMATICS

③ Smelling good? Stir in a cup or two of fresh or frozen bite-sized _____
VEG
in the order of how long they'll take to cook (harder vegetables like carrots go first so they have time to soften up; little softies like peas that'll cook quickly go last).

④ When your veg are tender, stir in the cooked or fast-cooking _____ .
PROTEIN
Keep stirring! Work those arm muscles!

⑤ As soon as everything has started to brown, crack in _____ eggs
NUMBER OF EATERS
and let them sit for a minute, just so they start to set, then give them a stir to scramble and cook up, 3 to 4 minutes total.

⑥ Add the cold cooked _____ —1 cup per eater—and a few
RICE OR GRAINS
tablespoons of _____ sauce.
SALTY/SPICY SAUCE

⑦ Stir everything around swiftly with a _____ until the grains are
UTENSIL
heated through and coated with sauce, about 5 minutes. If you like crispy bits, keep cooking until you get some charred spots.

⑧ Garnish with a flourish of chopped _____ . Grab chopsticks and
SOMETHING FRESH
eat out of _____ .
VESSEL

HINTS AND WINKS

RICE OR GRAINS
- long- or medium-grain white or brown rice
- farro
- quinoa
- barley
- freekeh

VEG
- carrots
- broccoli
- cabbage
- cauliflower
- peas

PROTEIN
- cooked ham
- leftover roast chicken
- grilled steak
- shrimp
- ground pork
- crumbled tofu

HIGH-SMOKE-POINT FAT
- canola, vegetable, or coconut oil

ALLIUMS
- white or red onions
- leeks

AROMATICS
- garlic
- ginger or lemongrass
- curry leaves

NUMBER OF EATERS
- anywhere from 4 to 6 (knock 'em dead!)

SALTY/SPICY SAUCE
- soy
- oyster
- teriyaki
- chili-garlic
- fish

UTENSIL
- wooden spoon
- spatula

SOMETHING FRESH
- scallions
- cilantro
- basil
- citrus zest

VESSEL
- the pan
- a mug
- a bowl
- a plate
- your hand

TIP

THE QUICKEST WAY TO COOKED RICE

Don't have any cold cooked rice on hand? Fear not! Here's the easiest way to get there. Rinse rice well, then cook it with a little less water than usual (use a ratio of 1 cup rice to 1½ cups water). When all the water has been absorbed, fluff the rice with a fork, spread it on a baking sheet, and leave it uncovered under a fan or in the fridge for at least a couple hours (or, hey, overnight), until it's mostly dry. At that point, it's ready for frying.

NOTES TO YOUR FUTURE SELF

_____

_____

_____

_____

_____

YIELD: 4 TO 6 SERVINGS

FRIED _____ WITH
RICE OR GRAINS

_____ & _____
VEG   PROTEIN

① Take a second to gather your thoughts and ingredients. This dish cooks quickly, so you'll want to make sure everything's chopped, prepped, and ready to rock and roll when you need it.

② Drag out a big skillet or wok and heat it over high heat for a minute, then swirl in a couple tablespoons of _____ . When the oil is shimmery-shiny, reduce
HIGH-SMOKE-POINT FAT
the heat to medium and add about 1 cup diced _____ and some
ALLIUMS
chopped/crushed _____ .
AROMATICS

③ Smelling good? Stir in a cup or two of fresh or frozen bite-sized _____
VEG
in the order of how long they'll take to cook (harder vegetables like carrots go first so they have time to soften up; little softies like peas that'll cook quickly go last).

④ When your veg are tender, stir in the cooked or fast-cooking _____ .
PROTEIN
Keep stirring! Work those arm muscles!

⑤ As soon as everything has started to brown, crack in _____ eggs
NUMBER OF EATERS
and let them sit for a minute, just so they start to set, then give them a stir to scramble and cook up, 3 to 4 minutes total.

⑥ Add the cold cooked _____ —1 cup per eater—and a few
RICE OR GRAINS
tablespoons of _____ sauce.
SALTY/SPICY SAUCE

⑦ Stir everything around swiftly with a _____ until the grains are
UTENSIL
heated through and coated with sauce, about 5 minutes. If you like crispy bits, keep cooking until you get some charred spots.

⑧ Garnish with a flourish of chopped _____ . Grab chopsticks and
SOMETHING FRESH
eat out of _____ .
VESSEL

HINTS AND WINKS

RICE OR GRAINS
- long- or medium-grain white or brown rice
- farro
- quinoa
- barley
- freekeh

VEG
- carrots
- broccoli
- cabbage
- cauliflower
- peas

PROTEIN
- cooked ham
- leftover roast chicken
- grilled steak
- shrimp
- ground pork
- crumbled tofu

HIGH-SMOKE-POINT FAT
- canola, vegetable, or coconut oil

ALLIUMS
- white or red onions
- leeks

AROMATICS
- garlic
- ginger or lemongrass
- curry leaves

NUMBER OF EATERS
- anywhere from 4 to 6 (knock 'em dead!)

SALTY/SPICY SAUCE
- soy
- oyster
- teriyaki
- chili-garlic
- fish

UTENSIL
- wooden spoon
- spatula

SOMETHING FRESH
- scallions
- cilantro
- basil
- citrus zest

VESSEL
- the pan
- a mug
- a bowl
- a plate
- your hand

TIP

THE QUICKEST WAY TO COOKED RICE

Don't have any cold cooked rice on hand? Fear not! Here's the easiest way to get there. Rinse rice well, then cook it with a little less water than usual (use a ratio of 1 cup rice to 1½ cups water). When all the water has been absorbed, fluff the rice with a fork, spread it on a baking sheet, and leave it uncovered under a fan or in the fridge for at least a couple hours (or, hey, overnight), until it's mostly dry. At that point, it's ready for frying.

NOTES TO YOUR FUTURE SELF

_____

_____

_____

_____

_____

FRIED _____ WITH
RICE OR GRAINS

_____ & _____
VEG   PROTEIN

① Take a second to gather your thoughts and ingredients. This dish cooks quickly, so you'll want to make sure everything's chopped, prepped, and ready to rock and roll when you need it.

② Drag out a big skillet or wok and heat it over high heat for a minute, then swirl in a couple tablespoons of _____ . When the oil is shimmery-shiny, reduce
HIGH-SMOKE-POINT FAT

the heat to medium and add about 1 cup diced _____ and some
ALLIUMS

chopped/crushed _____ .
AROMATICS

③ Smelling good? Stir in a cup or two of fresh or frozen bite-sized _____
VEG

in the order of how long they'll take to cook (harder vegetables like carrots go first so they have time to soften up; little softies like peas that'll cook quickly go last).

④ When your veg are tender, stir in the cooked or fast-cooking _____ .
PROTEIN

Keep stirring! Work those arm muscles!

⑤ As soon as everything has started to brown, crack in _____ eggs
NUMBER OF EATERS

and let them sit for a minute, just so they start to set, then give them a stir to scramble and cook up, 3 to 4 minutes total.

⑥ Add the cold cooked _____ —1 cup per eater—and a few
RICE OR GRAINS

tablespoons of _____ sauce.
SALTY/SPICY SAUCE

⑦ Stir everything around swiftly with a _____ until the grains are
UTENSIL

heated through and coated with sauce, about 5 minutes. If you like crispy bits, keep cooking until you get some charred spots.

⑧ Garnish with a flourish of chopped _____ . Grab chopsticks and
SOMETHING FRESH

eat out of _____ .
VESSEL

HINTS AND WINKS

RICE OR GRAINS
- long- or medium-grain white or brown rice
- farro
- quinoa
- barley
- freekeh

VEG
- carrots
- broccoli
- cabbage
- cauliflower
- peas

PROTEIN
- cooked ham
- leftover roast chicken
- grilled steak
- shrimp
- ground pork
- crumbled tofu

HIGH-SMOKE-POINT FAT
- canola, vegetable, or coconut oil

ALLIUMS
- white or red onions
- leeks

AROMATICS
- garlic
- ginger or lemongrass
- curry leaves

NUMBER OF EATERS
- anywhere from 4 to 6 (knock 'em dead!)

SALTY/SPICY SAUCE
- soy
- oyster
- teriyaki
- chili-garlic
- fish

UTENSIL
- wooden spoon
- spatula

SOMETHING FRESH
- scallions
- cilantro
- basil
- citrus zest

VESSEL
- the pan
- a mug
- a bowl
- a plate
- your hand

TIP

THE QUICKEST WAY TO COOKED RICE

Don't have any cold cooked rice on hand? Fear not! Here's the easiest way to get there. Rinse rice well, then cook it with a little less water than usual (use a ratio of 1 cup rice to 1½ cups water). When all the water has been absorbed, fluff the rice with a fork, spread it on a baking sheet, and leave it uncovered under a fan or in the fridge for at least a couple hours (or, hey, overnight), until it's mostly dry. At that point, it's ready for frying.

NOTES TO YOUR FUTURE SELF

_____

_____

_____

_____

_____

COZY STEWED _____
TYPE OF BEANS

BEANS & _____ GREENS
TYPE OF GREENS

① Warm some _____ in a large pot or Dutch oven over medium
COOKING FAT

heat. The chillier and more blustery the weather, the more fat you'll want.

② If you'd like, add up to ½ pound chopped _____ . When the
SOMETHING SAVORY

contents of the pan become crispy and golden and splendid, strain them out and set

them aside.

③ Sauté some chopped _____ in the fat over medium heat,
ALLIUMS

or bump the heat down and caramelize them low and slow. When they're nearly

done, add some _____ and a teaspoon or two of
AROMATICS

_____ . Toast for a minute or two, just till they start to
SPICES

smell great.

④ Pour in a splash of _____ and use a spoon to scrape up any
BOOZE

browned bits from the bottom of the pot, then follow up with at least 3 cups stock

or water. For something a little more rib-sticking, swirl in up to 1 cup of

_____ . Take a taste and start tinkering with the flavor:
SOMETHING CREAMY

add a teaspoon of _____ or salt and a tablespoon of
HEAT

_____ at a time.
ACID

⑤ Let the broth come to a simmer, then add a few cups canned or cooked

_____ beans and let them warm through.
TYPE OF BEANS

⑥ Tumble in the stemmed, chopped _____ greens, of which you'll
TYPE OF GREENS

want at least 2 cups total. Cook them to tenderness but not oblivion—heartier greens will

need a few minutes, while delicate ones can go in right as you're turning off the heat.

⑦ Put some cooked _____ in the bottom of a deep, warm bowl and
SOMETHING CARB-Y

ladle the stew over it with _____ . Eat with your biggest spoon.
A NICE AFTERTHOUGHT

HINTS AND WINKS

TYPE OF BEANS
- white
- red
- black
- lima

TYPE OF GREENS
- collard
- mustard
- turnip
- beet
- dandelion

COOKING FAT
- butter or ghee
- olive or coconut oil
- pork or bacon fat
- schmaltz

SOMETHING SAVORY
- pancetta or bacon
- sausage
- ham
- mushrooms

ALLIUMS
- red or yellow onions
- leeks
- shallots

AROMATICS
- minced ginger or lemongrass
- garlic
- tomato paste
- anchovies
- bay leaves

SPICES
- curry, chili, or five-spice powder
- garam masala
- Aleppo pepper

BOOZE
- red or white wine
- sherry or vermouth
- beer

SOMETHING CREAMY
- heavy cream
- coconut milk

HEAT
- red pepper flakes
- adobo sauce
- sambal

ACID
- vinegar (balsamic, cider, sherry, wine)
- lemon juice

SOMETHING CARB-Y
- toast
- cooked polenta or grits
- farro
- egg noodles

A NICE AFTERTHOUGHT
- olive oil
- more acid
- soy sauce
- sriracha
- crispy bread crumbs

NOTES TO YOUR FUTURE SELF

_____

_____

_____

_____

_____

COZY STEWED _____
TYPE OF BEANS

BEANS & _____ GREENS
TYPE OF GREENS

① Warm some _____ in a large pot or Dutch oven over medium
COOKING FAT

heat. The chillier and more blustery the weather, the more fat you'll want.

② If you'd like, add up to ½ pound chopped _____ . When the
SOMETHING SAVORY

contents of the pan become crispy and golden and splendid, strain them out and set

them aside.

③ Sauté some chopped _____ in the fat over medium heat,
ALLIUMS

or bump the heat down and caramelize them low and slow. When they're nearly

done, add some _____ and a teaspoon or two of
AROMATICS

_____ . Toast for a minute or two, just till they start to
SPICES

smell great.

④ Pour in a splash of _____ and use a spoon to scrape up any
BOOZE

browned bits from the bottom of the pot, then follow up with at least 3 cups stock

or water. For something a little more rib-sticking, swirl in up to 1 cup of

_____ . Take a taste and start tinkering with the flavor:
SOMETHING CREAMY

add a teaspoon of _____ or salt and a tablespoon of
HEAT

_____ at a time.
ACID

⑤ Let the broth come to a simmer, then add a few cups canned or cooked

_____ beans and let them warm through.
TYPE OF BEANS

⑥ Tumble in the stemmed, chopped _____ greens, of which you'll
TYPE OF GREENS

want at least 2 cups total. Cook them to tenderness but not oblivion—heartier greens will

need a few minutes, while delicate ones can go in right as you're turning off the heat.

⑦ Put some cooked _____ in the bottom of a deep, warm bowl and
SOMETHING CARB-Y

ladle the stew over it with _____ . Eat with your biggest spoon.
A NICE AFTERTHOUGHT

HINTS AND WINKS

TYPE OF BEANS
- white
- red
- black
- lima

TYPE OF GREENS
- collard
- mustard
- turnip
- beet
- dandelion

COOKING FAT
- butter or ghee
- olive or coconut oil
- pork or bacon fat
- schmaltz

SOMETHING SAVORY
- pancetta or bacon
- sausage
- ham
- mushrooms

ALLIUMS
- red or yellow onions
- leeks
- shallots

AROMATICS
- minced ginger or lemongrass
- garlic
- tomato paste
- anchovies
- bay leaves

SPICES
- curry, chili, or five-spice powder
- garam masala
- Aleppo pepper

BOOZE
- red or white wine
- sherry or vermouth
- beer

SOMETHING CREAMY
- heavy cream
- coconut milk

HEAT
- red pepper flakes
- adobo sauce
- sambal

ACID
- vinegar (balsamic, cider, sherry, wine)
- lemon juice

SOMETHING CARB-Y
- toast
- cooked polenta or grits
- farro
- egg noodles

A NICE AFTERTHOUGHT
- olive oil
- more acid
- soy sauce
- sriracha
- crispy bread crumbs

TIP

THE QUICKEST WAY TO COOK DRY BEANS

Forgot an overnight soak? No worries—give them a jump-start in about as much time as it'll take you to walk the dog, shower, and change into freshly washed jeans. Put the beans in your biggest pot and add water to cover. Bring the whole thing up to a boil, let 'em rip for a minute, then turn off the heat, cover the pot, and leave them alone for an hour. When you come back to the pot, cook them as you would if you'd started them yesterday.

NOTES TO YOUR FUTURE SELF

_____

_____

_____

_____

_____

COZY STEWED _____
TYPE OF BEANS

BEANS & _____ GREENS
TYPE OF GREENS

① Warm some _____ in a large pot or Dutch oven over medium
COOKING FAT

heat. The chillier and more blustery the weather, the more fat you'll want.

② If you'd like, add up to ½ pound chopped _____ . When the
SOMETHING SAVORY

contents of the pan become crispy and golden and splendid, strain them out and set

them aside.

③ Sauté some chopped _____ in the fat over medium heat,
ALLIUMS

or bump the heat down and caramelize them low and slow. When they're nearly

done, add some _____ and a teaspoon or two of
AROMATICS

_____ . Toast for a minute or two, just till they start to
SPICES

smell great.

④ Pour in a splash of _____ and use a spoon to scrape up any
BOOZE

browned bits from the bottom of the pot, then follow up with at least 3 cups stock

or water. For something a little more rib-sticking, swirl in up to 1 cup of

_____ . Take a taste and start tinkering with the flavor:
SOMETHING CREAMY

add a teaspoon of _____ or salt and a tablespoon of
HEAT

_____ at a time.
ACID

⑤ Let the broth come to a simmer, then add a few cups canned or cooked

_____ beans and let them warm through.
TYPE OF BEANS

⑥ Tumble in the stemmed, chopped _____ greens, of which you'll
TYPE OF GREENS

want at least 2 cups total. Cook them to tenderness but not oblivion—heartier greens will

need a few minutes, while delicate ones can go in right as you're turning off the heat.

⑦ Put some cooked _____ in the bottom of a deep, warm bowl and
SOMETHING CARB-Y

ladle the stew over it with _____ . Eat with your biggest spoon.
A NICE AFTERTHOUGHT

HINTS AND WINKS

TYPE OF BEANS
- white
- red
- black
- lima

TYPE OF GREENS
- collard
- mustard
- turnip
- beet
- dandelion

COOKING FAT
- butter or ghee
- olive or coconut oil
- pork or bacon fat
- schmaltz

SOMETHING SAVORY
- pancetta or bacon
- sausage
- ham
- mushrooms

ALLIUMS
- red or yellow onions
- leeks
- shallots

AROMATICS
- minced ginger or lemongrass
- garlic
- tomato paste
- anchovies
- bay leaves

SPICES
- curry, chili, or five-spice powder
- garam masala
- Aleppo pepper

BOOZE
- red or white wine
- sherry or vermouth
- beer

SOMETHING CREAMY
- heavy cream
- coconut milk

HEAT
- red pepper flakes
- adobo sauce
- sambal

ACID
- vinegar (balsamic, cider, sherry, wine)
- lemon juice

SOMETHING CARB-Y
- toast
- cooked polenta or grits
- farro
- egg noodles

A NICE AFTERTHOUGHT
- olive oil
- more acid
- soy sauce
- sriracha
- crispy bread crumbs

TIP

THE QUICKEST WAY TO COOK DRY BEANS

Forgot an overnight soak? No worries—give them a jump-start in about as much time as it'll take you to walk the dog, shower, and change into freshly washed jeans. Put the beans in your biggest pot and add water to cover. Bring the whole thing up to a boil, let 'em rip for a minute, then turn off the heat, cover the pot, and leave them alone for an hour. When you come back to the pot, cook them as you would if you'd started them yesterday.

NOTES TO YOUR FUTURE SELF

_____-CRUSTED
SOMETHING CRISPY
CHICKEN TENDERS

1. If you're baking your tenders, preheat the oven to 400°F. Line a rimmed baking sheet with parchment paper or foil. (If you're pan-frying, skip all this and hold tight till step 4.)

2. Cut about 1½ pounds boneless, skinless chicken breasts into 1¼-inch-wide strips. Stick them in a zip-top bag with _____ and set aside to marinate for
   YOUR FAVORITE MARINADE
   about 30 minutes. Or don't—you're the boss of you!

3. In a wide, shallow bowl, combine a cup or so of all-purpose flour with a two-finger pinch of salt and a tablespoon or two of _____ . In another wide,
   SPICES
   shallow bowl, beat 2 eggs. Grab a third bowl and fill it with 2 cups fine bread crumbs or
   _____ (finely crushed or shredded, as needed). Add a fistful
   SOMETHING CRISPY
   of _____ , if the spirit moves you.
   SWANKY EXTRAS

4. If you're pan-frying the chicken, now's the time to pour enough
   _____ oil into a large, heavy skillet to fill the bottom. Set the
   COOKING OIL
   pan over medium-high heat and let the oil get shimmery. Line a plate with paper towels.

5. Dredge each piece of chicken through the flour, dip into the eggs, and finally coat evenly with the bread crumbs. Arrange the coated pieces on the prepared baking sheet or in the hot skillet in a noncrowded fashion and cook until each piece is deep golden all over, 6 to 8 minutes per side in the oven, or 2 to 3 minutes per side on the stove. If you're frying the tenders, transfer them to the towel-lined plate to drain.

6. Dunk the chicken in _____ and enjoy, accompanied by
   SOME TASTY DIP
   _____ .
   YOUR FAVORITE '90S SITCOM

HINTS AND WINKS

SOMETHING CRISPY
- panko
- cornmeal
- potato chips
- coconut

YOUR FAVORITE MARINADE
- soy sauce with sliced ginger
- buttermilk
- red pepper flakes with lime
- something with hot sauce

SPICES
- black pepper
- cayenne pepper
- ground cumin
- smoked paprika
- chili or curry powder
- za'atar

SWANKY EXTRAS
- grated Parmesan or pecorino
- sesame seeds
- furikake

COOKING OIL
- olive, canola, or coconut

SOME TASTY DIP
- honey mustard
- barbecue sauce
- herbed mayonnaise
- sriracha ketchup
- blue cheese dip

YOUR FAVORITE '90s SITCOM
- *Murphy Brown*
- *The Fresh Prince of Bel-Air*
- *Full House*
- *The Nanny*

TIP

DON'T HAVE CRUMBS? IMPROVISE!

Combine the **seasoned flour** from step 3 with a little less than **1 cup water or buttermilk**. Swipe the chicken through this mixture until it's completely coated, then get right to frying.

NOTES TO YOUR FUTURE SELF

_____-CRUSTED
SOMETHING CRISPY
CHICKEN TENDERS

① If you're baking your tenders, preheat the oven to 400°F. Line a rimmed baking sheet with parchment paper or foil. (If you're pan-frying, skip all this and hold tight till step 4.)

② Cut about 1½ pounds boneless, skinless chicken breasts into 1¼-inch-wide strips. Stick them in a zip-top bag with _____ and set aside to marinate for
YOUR FAVORITE MARINADE
about 30 minutes. Or don't—you're the boss of you!

③ In a wide, shallow bowl, combine a cup or so of all-purpose flour with a two-finger pinch of salt and a tablespoon or two of _____ . In another wide,
SPICES
shallow bowl, beat 2 eggs. Grab a third bowl and fill it with 2 cups fine bread crumbs or
_____ (finely crushed or shredded, as needed). Add a fistful
SOMETHING CRISPY
of _____ , if the spirit moves you.
SWANKY EXTRAS

④ If you're pan-frying the chicken, now's the time to pour enough
_____ oil into a large, heavy skillet to fill the bottom. Set the
COOKING OIL
pan over medium-high heat and let the oil get shimmery. Line a plate with paper towels.

⑤ Dredge each piece of chicken through the flour, dip into the eggs, and finally coat evenly with the bread crumbs. Arrange the coated pieces on the prepared baking sheet or in the hot skillet in a noncrowded fashion and cook until each piece is deep golden all over, 6 to 8 minutes per side in the oven, or 2 to 3 minutes per side on the stove. If you're frying the tenders, transfer them to the towel-lined plate to drain.

⑥ Dunk the chicken in _____ and enjoy, accompanied by
SOME TASTY DIP
_____ .
YOUR FAVORITE '90S SITCOM

HINTS AND WINKS

SOMETHING CRISPY
- panko
- cornmeal
- potato chips
- coconut

YOUR FAVORITE MARINADE
- soy sauce with sliced ginger
- buttermilk
- red pepper flakes with lime
- something with hot sauce

SPICES
- black pepper
- cayenne pepper
- ground cumin
- smoked paprika
- chili or curry powder
- za'atar

SWANKY EXTRAS
- grated Parmesan
  or pecorino
- sesame seeds
- furikake

COOKING OIL
- olive, canola, or coconut

SOME TASTY DIP
- honey mustard
- barbecue sauce
- herbed mayonnaise
- sriracha ketchup
- blue cheese dip

YOUR FAVORITE '90s SITCOM
- *Murphy Brown*
- *The Fresh Prince of Bel-Air*
- *Full House*
- *The Nanny*

TIP

DON'T HAVE CRUMBS? IMPROVISE!

Combine the **seasoned flour** from step 3 with a little less than **1 cup water or buttermilk**. Swipe the chicken through this mixture until it's completely coated, then get right to frying.

NOTES TO YOUR FUTURE SELF

_____

_____

_____

_____

_____

_____-CRUSTED
SOMETHING CRISPY
CHICKEN TENDERS

① If you're baking your tenders, preheat the oven to 400°F. Line a rimmed baking sheet with parchment paper or foil. (If you're pan-frying, skip all this and hold tight till step 4.)

② Cut about 1½ pounds boneless, skinless chicken breasts into 1¼-inch-wide strips. Stick them in a zip-top bag with _____ and set aside to marinate for
YOUR FAVORITE MARINADE
about 30 minutes. Or don't—you're the boss of you!

③ In a wide, shallow bowl, combine a cup or so of all-purpose flour with a two-finger pinch of salt and a tablespoon or two of _____ . In another wide,
SPICES
shallow bowl, beat 2 eggs. Grab a third bowl and fill it with 2 cups fine bread crumbs or
_____ (finely crushed or shredded, as needed). Add a fistful
SOMETHING CRISPY
of _____ , if the spirit moves you.
SWANKY EXTRAS

④ If you're pan-frying the chicken, now's the time to pour enough
_____ oil into a large, heavy skillet to fill the bottom. Set the
COOKING OIL
pan over medium-high heat and let the oil get shimmery. Line a plate with paper towels.

⑤ Dredge each piece of chicken through the flour, dip into the eggs, and finally coat evenly with the bread crumbs. Arrange the coated pieces on the prepared baking sheet or in the hot skillet in a noncrowded fashion and cook until each piece is deep golden all over, 6 to 8 minutes per side in the oven, or 2 to 3 minutes per side on the stove. If you're frying the tenders, transfer them to the towel-lined plate to drain.

⑥ Dunk the chicken in _____ and enjoy, accompanied by
SOME TASTY DIP
_____ .
YOUR FAVORITE '90S SITCOM

HINTS AND WINKS

SOMETHING CRISPY
- panko
- cornmeal
- potato chips
- coconut

YOUR FAVORITE MARINADE
- soy sauce with sliced ginger
- buttermilk
- red pepper flakes with lime
- something with hot sauce

SPICES
- black pepper
- cayenne pepper
- ground cumin
- smoked paprika
- chili or curry powder
- za'atar

SWANKY EXTRAS
- grated Parmesan or pecorino
- sesame seeds
- furikake

COOKING OIL
- olive, canola, or coconut

SOME TASTY DIP
- honey mustard
- barbecue sauce
- herbed mayonnaise
- sriracha ketchup
- blue cheese dip

YOUR FAVORITE '90s SITCOM
- *Murphy Brown*
- *The Fresh Prince of Bel-Air*
- *Full House*
- *The Nanny*

TIP

DON'T HAVE CRUMBS? IMPROVISE!

Combine the **seasoned flour** from step 3 with a little less than **1 cup water or buttermilk**. Swipe the chicken through this mixture until it's completely coated, then get right to frying.

NOTES TO YOUR FUTURE SELF

_____

_____

_____

_____

_____

YIELD: ABOUT 8 SERVINGS

_____   _____
SOOTHING ADJECTIVE   SUBSTANTIAL FILLING

LASAGNA

① Preheat the oven to 400°F. Lightly grease a large rectangular baking dish with

_____ .
　　　COOKING FAT

② Prepare your _____ . You'll need enough for about four layers.
　　　　　　　NOODLES OR OTHERWISE

If the pasta has to be parcooked, drop it in boiling water and remove it about a minute

before it's al dente. If you're using zucchini or eggplant, salt it and let it drain for about

15 minutes, then roast it until it's lightly browned.

③ The work of a lasagna is in the assembly, so take a minute to *mise* your *place* and get

everything set up. Rustle up a few good-sized bowls to hold all the components: one for

noodles, one or two for sauces, one for grated cheese, and one for each of your extras.

④ Fill one bowl with a few cups of _____ and another with an
　　　　　　　　　　　　　　CREAMY SAUCE

equal amount of _____ (or skip the former and double down on
　　　　　　　SUBSTANTIAL FILLING

the latter). Fill a third bowl with some grated _____ cheese.
　　　　　　　　　　　　　　　　　TYPE OF CHEESE

⑤ Tile the noodles on the bottom of the baking dish without letting them overlap and

top with a thin smattering of your _____ and a modest heap of
　　　　　　　　　　　　　CREAMY SAUCE

_____ , followed by a snowfall of _____
　SUBSTANTIAL FILLING　　　　　　　　　　　　　　　TYPE OF CHEESE

cheese. If you've got _____ , throw some over each layer of cheese.
　　　　　　　　EXTRAS

⑥ . Continue this pattern until the _____ is all gone. Top with a ceiling
　　　　　　　　　　　　　SUBSTANTIAL FILLING

of noodles, _____ , and grated _____ cheese.
　　　　　CREAMY SAUCE　　　　　　　　　　TYPE OF CHEESE

Bake for 20 to 30 minutes, until the top is browned and gently bubbling. Put it under

the broiler at the very end to bump up the drama: more bubbles, more browning.

⑦ Stare at your lasagna lovingly, or otherwise keep yourself occupied, for 5 or 10 minutes

so it can set up. Feed a crowd—or just feed yourself from the freezer for a month!

Leftover lasagna is killer when it's pan-fried on its side.

HINTS AND WINKS

SOOTHING ADJECTIVE
- melty
- gooey
- bubbling
- easy

SUBSTANTIAL FILLING
- Bolognese
- roasted squash
- spinach

COOKING FAT
- butter or ghee
- olive oil
- pork or bacon fat

NOODLES OR OTHERWISE
- actual lasagna noodles
- very thinly sliced zucchini or eggplant

CREAMY SAUCE
- **Béchamel**
- ricotta
- whipped cottage cheese

TYPE OF CHEESE
- Parmesan
- pecorino
- ricotta salata
- mozzarella
- Gruyère

EXTRAS
- mortadella
- prosciutto
- ham
- cooked sausage or meatballs

BÉCHAMEL

Melt ½ **cup (1 stick) butter** in a large skillet over medium heat, then stir in ½ **cup all-purpose flour** and whisk continuously until it's a pale blond color. Little by little, whisk in **4 cups whole milk or half-and-half**. Stir idly and wait patiently—it'll thicken after 8 to 10 minutes. Season with **salt** and **freshly ground black pepper** and you're good to go.

NOTES TO YOUR FUTURE SELF

YIELD: ABOUT 8 SERVINGS

_____ _____
SOOTHING ADJECTIVE   SUBSTANTIAL FILLING

LASAGNA

① Preheat the oven to 400°F. Lightly grease a large rectangular baking dish with

_____ .
COOKING FAT

② Prepare your _____ . You'll need enough for about four layers.
NOODLES OR OTHERWISE

If the pasta has to be parcooked, drop it in boiling water and remove it about a minute

before it's al dente. If you're using zucchini or eggplant, salt it and let it drain for about

15 minutes, then roast it until it's lightly browned.

③ The work of a lasagna is in the assembly, so take a minute to *mise* your *place* and get

everything set up. Rustle up a few good-sized bowls to hold all the components: one for

noodles, one or two for sauces, one for grated cheese, and one for each of your extras.

④ Fill one bowl with a few cups of _____ and another with an
CREAMY SAUCE

equal amount of _____ (or skip the former and double down on
SUBSTANTIAL FILLING

the latter). Fill a third bowl with some grated _____ cheese.
TYPE OF CHEESE

⑤ Tile the noodles on the bottom of the baking dish without letting them overlap and

top with a thin smattering of your _____ and a modest heap of
CREAMY SAUCE

_____ , followed by a snowfall of _____
SUBSTANTIAL FILLING   TYPE OF CHEESE

cheese. If you've got _____ , throw some over each layer of cheese.
EXTRAS

⑥ Continue this pattern until the _____ is all gone. Top with a ceiling
SUBSTANTIAL FILLING

of noodles, _____ , and grated _____ cheese.
CREAMY SAUCE   TYPE OF CHEESE

Bake for 20 to 30 minutes, until the top is browned and gently bubbling. Put it under

the broiler at the very end to bump up the drama: more bubbles, more browning.

⑦ Stare at your lasagna lovingly, or otherwise keep yourself occupied, for 5 or 10 minutes

so it can set up. Feed a crowd—or just feed yourself from the freezer for a month!

Leftover lasagna is killer when it's pan-fried on its side.

HINTS AND WINKS

SOOTHING ADJECTIVE
- melty
- gooey
- bubbling
- easy

SUBSTANTIAL FILLING
- Bolognese
- roasted squash
- spinach

COOKING FAT
- butter or ghee
- olive oil
- pork or bacon fat

NOODLES OR OTHERWISE
- actual lasagna noodles
- very thinly sliced zucchini or eggplant

CREAMY SAUCE
- **Béchamel**
- ricotta
- whipped cottage cheese

TYPE OF CHEESE
- Parmesan
- pecorino
- ricotta salata
- mozzarella
- Gruyère

EXTRAS
- mortadella
- prosciutto
- ham
- cooked sausage or meatballs

BÉCHAMEL

Melt ½ **cup (1 stick) butter** in a large skillet over medium heat, then stir in ½ **cup all-purpose flour** and whisk continuously until it's a pale blond color. Little by little, whisk in **4 cups whole milk or half-and-half**. Stir idly and wait patiently—it'll thicken after 8 to 10 minutes. Season with **salt** and **freshly ground black pepper** and you're good to go.

NOTES TO YOUR FUTURE SELF

_____   _____
SOOTHING ADJECTIVE   SUBSTANTIAL FILLING

LASAGNA

① Preheat the oven to 400°F. Lightly grease a large rectangular baking dish with

_____ .
COOKING FAT

② Prepare your _____ . You'll need enough for about four layers.
NOODLES OR OTHERWISE

If the pasta has to be parcooked, drop it in boiling water and remove it about a minute

before it's al dente. If you're using zucchini or eggplant, salt it and let it drain for about

15 minutes, then roast it until it's lightly browned.

③ The work of a lasagna is in the assembly, so take a minute to *mise* your *place* and get

everything set up. Rustle up a few good-sized bowls to hold all the components: one for

noodles, one or two for sauces, one for grated cheese, and one for each of your extras.

④ Fill one bowl with a few cups of _____ and another with an
CREAMY SAUCE

equal amount of _____ (or skip the former and double down on
SUBSTANTIAL FILLING

the latter). Fill a third bowl with some grated _____ cheese.
TYPE OF CHEESE

⑤ Tile the noodles on the bottom of the baking dish without letting them overlap and

top with a thin smattering of your _____ and a modest heap of
CREAMY SAUCE

_____ , followed by a snowfall of _____
SUBSTANTIAL FILLING   TYPE OF CHEESE

cheese. If you've got _____ , throw some over each layer of cheese.
EXTRAS

⑥ Continue this pattern until the _____ is all gone. Top with a ceiling
SUBSTANTIAL FILLING

of noodles, _____ , and grated _____ cheese.
CREAMY SAUCE   TYPE OF CHEESE

Bake for 20 to 30 minutes, until the top is browned and gently bubbling. Put it under

the broiler at the very end to bump up the drama: more bubbles, more browning.

⑦ Stare at your lasagna lovingly, or otherwise keep yourself occupied, for 5 or 10 minutes

so it can set up. Feed a crowd—or just feed yourself from the freezer for a month!

Leftover lasagna is killer when it's pan-fried on its side.

HINTS AND WINKS

SOOTHING ADJECTIVE
- melty
- gooey
- bubbling
- easy

SUBSTANTIAL FILLING
- Bolognese
- roasted squash
- spinach

COOKING FAT
- butter or ghee
- olive oil
- pork or bacon fat

NOODLES OR OTHERWISE
- actual lasagna noodles
- very thinly sliced zucchini or eggplant

CREAMY SAUCE
- **Béchamel**
- ricotta
- whipped cottage cheese

TYPE OF CHEESE
- Parmesan
- pecorino
- ricotta salata
- mozzarella
- Gruyère

EXTRAS
- mortadella
- prosciutto
- ham
- cooked sausage or meatballs

WHIP IT UP

BÉCHAMEL

Melt ½ **cup (1 stick) butter** in a large skillet over medium heat, then stir in ½ **cup all-purpose flour** and whisk continuously until it's a pale blond color. Little by little, whisk in **4 cups whole milk or half-and-half**. Stir idly and wait patiently—it'll thicken after 8 to 10 minutes. Season with **salt** and **freshly ground black pepper** and you're good to go.

NOTES TO YOUR FUTURE SELF

LOVER'S BOWL

_____
POPULAR WELLNESS PURSUIT

_____
TYPE OF GRAINS

① Spread a good scoop of cooked _____ over the bottom of
                                        TYPE OF GRAINS

your favorite, friendliest single-serving bowl (if you've got company, make one of these

for each eater).

② Add a scoop of _____ to one quadrant and a scoop of
                          RAW VEGETABLES

_____ to another. (If you prefer to commingle your ingredients,
      COOKED VEGETABLES

go right ahead.)

③ Fill any empty space with _____ and snuggle in a
                                    COOKED PROTEIN

_____ egg, while you're at it.
      EGG-COOKING METHOD

④ Now, let the dressing rain down! If you want something light and fresh, go with

_____ ; if you're looking for something creamy and
      DRESSING THAT'LL MAKE YOU BOP AROUND

comforting, choose _____ .
                          DRESSING THAT'LL TUCK YOU INTO BED

⑤ Don't forget to garnish: wisps of _____ ,
                                          FRUITS, VEGETABLES, PICKLES

_____ cheese, some _____ , and
      TYPE OF CHEESE   FRESH HERBS

_____ . Finish with some sliced or smashed avocado—this is a
      NUTS & SEEDS

grain bowl, after all.

HINTS AND WINKS

POPULAR WELLNESS PURSUIT
- yoga
- Pilates
- meditation
- spin class

TYPE OF GRAINS
- freekeh
- farro or wheat berries
- quinoa
- couscous
- polenta or grits
- leftover take-out rice

RAW VEGETABLES
- shaved carrots
- shredded Brussels sprouts
- slivered bell pepper
- handful of leafy greens

COOKED VEGETABLES
- roasted squash
- roasted or steamed cauliflower or broccoli
- braised or oil-poached mushrooms

COOKED PROTEIN
- canned tuna or salmon
- roasted or poached chicken
- sautéed shrimp
- bacon
- braised tempeh or tofu

EGG-COOKING METHOD
- poached
- fried
- soft- or hard-boiled
- pickled

DRESSING THAT'LL MAKE YOU BOP AROUND
- miso dressing
- balsamic vinaigrette
- chimichurri

DRESSING THAT'LL TUCK YOU INTO BED
- buttermilk ranch
- green goddess
- bacon vinaigrette
- blue cheese

FRUITS, VEGETABLES, PICKLES
- shaved or julienned apple
- persimmon or pear slices
- cucumber slices
- **Quick-Pickled Vegetables**

TYPE OF CHEESE
- ricotta
- blue
- goat
- feta
- Parmesan

FRESH HERBS
- dill
- basil
- chervil
- mint

NUTS & SEEDS
- almonds or walnuts
- sesame seeds
- furikake

QUICK-PICKLED VEGETABLES

Gather **1 pound assorted vegetables**—carrots, cucumbers, summer squash, radishes, jalapeños, cauliflower, and onions are surefire bets. Cut them into spears or slices and pack them into a big glass jar (since you're not doing this for long-term preservation, it doesn't have to be sterilized, but make sure it's squeaky clean). Make a brine with **1 cup water, 1 cup vinegar** (distilled white, cider, or rice), up to **¼ cup kosher salt,** up to ¼ **cup sugar,** and any **whole spices** (bay leaves, sliced fresh ginger, red pepper flakes, mustard seeds) and **fresh herbs** (dill, oregano, cilantro) that are calling your name. If your veg are delicate enough for, say, a crudité platter, you can leave the brine cold; otherwise, bring it to an active simmer in a saucepan. Pour it directly into the jar, filling the jar all the way up to the top and making sure all the veg are submerged. Cover and refrigerate overnight for round-the-clock garnishing (and snacking).

NOTES TO YOUR FUTURE SELF

_____

_____

_____

_____

_____

_____ LOVER'S
POPULAR WELLNESS PURSUIT

_____ BOWL
TYPE OF GRAINS

① Spread a good scoop of cooked _____ over the bottom of
TYPE OF GRAINS

your favorite, friendliest single-serving bowl (if you've got company, make one of these

for each eater).

② Add a scoop of _____ to one quadrant and a scoop of
RAW VEGETABLES

_____ to another. (If you prefer to commingle your ingredients,
COOKED VEGETABLES

go right ahead.)

③ Fill any empty space with _____ and snuggle in a
COOKED PROTEIN

_____ egg, while you're at it.
EGG-COOKING METHOD

④ Now, let the dressing rain down! If you want something light and fresh, go with

_____ ; if you're looking for something creamy and
DRESSING THAT'LL MAKE YOU BOP AROUND

comforting, choose _____ .
DRESSING THAT'LL TUCK YOU INTO BED

⑤ Don't forget to garnish: wisps of _____ ,
FRUITS, VEGETABLES, PICKLES

_____ cheese, some _____ , and
TYPE OF CHEESE   FRESH HERBS

_____ . Finish with some sliced or smashed avocado—this is a
NUTS & SEEDS

grain bowl, after all.

HINTS AND WINKS

POPULAR WELLNESS PURSUIT

- yoga
- Pilates
- meditation
- spin class

TYPE OF GRAINS

- freekeh
- farro or wheat berries
- quinoa
- couscous
- polenta or grits
- leftover take-out rice

RAW VEGETABLES

- shaved carrots
- shredded Brussels sprouts
- slivered bell pepper
- handful of leafy greens

COOKED VEGETABLES

- roasted squash
- roasted or steamed cauliflower or broccoli
- braised or oil-poached mushrooms

COOKED PROTEIN

- canned tuna or salmon
- roasted or poached chicken
- sautéed shrimp
- bacon
- braised tempeh or tofu

EGG-COOKING METHOD

- poached
- fried
- soft- or hard-boiled
- pickled

DRESSING THAT'LL MAKE YOU BOP AROUND

- miso dressing
- balsamic vinaigrette
- chimichurri

DRESSING THAT'LL TUCK YOU INTO BED

- buttermilk ranch
- green goddess
- bacon vinaigrette
- blue cheese

FRUITS, VEGETABLES, PICKLES

- shaved or julienned apple
- persimmon or pear slices
- cucumber slices
- **Quick-Pickled Vegetables**

TYPE OF CHEESE

- ricotta
- blue
- goat
- feta
- Parmesan

FRESH HERBS

- dill
- basil
- chervil
- mint

NUTS & SEEDS

- almonds or walnuts
- sesame seeds
- furikake

WHIP IT UP

QUICK-PICKLED VEGETABLES

Gather **1 pound assorted vegetables**—carrots, cucumbers, summer squash, radishes, jalapeños, cauliflower, and onions are surefire bets. Cut them into spears or slices and pack them into a big glass jar (since you're not doing this for long-term preservation, it doesn't have to be sterilized, but make sure it's squeaky clean). Make a brine with **1 cup water, 1 cup vinegar** (distilled white, cider, or rice), up to **¼ cup kosher salt,** up to **¼ cup sugar,** and any **whole spices** (bay leaves, sliced fresh ginger, red pepper flakes, mustard seeds) and **fresh herbs** (dill, oregano, cilantro) that are calling your name. If your veg are delicate enough for, say, a crudité platter, you can leave the brine cold; otherwise, bring it to an active simmer in a saucepan. Pour it directly into the jar, filling the jar all the way up to the top and making sure all the veg are submerged. Cover and refrigerate overnight for round-the-clock garnishing (and snacking).

NOTES TO YOUR FUTURE SELF

_____

_____

_____

_____

_____

_____ **LOVER'S**
POPULAR WELLNESS PURSUIT

_____ **BOWL**
TYPE OF GRAINS

① Spread a good scoop of cooked _____ over the bottom of
TYPE OF GRAINS

your favorite, friendliest single-serving bowl (if you've got company, make one of these

for each eater).

② Add a scoop of _____ to one quadrant and a scoop of
RAW VEGETABLES

_____ to another. (If you prefer to commingle your ingredients,
COOKED VEGETABLES

go right ahead.)

③ Fill any empty space with _____ and snuggle in a
COOKED PROTEIN

_____ egg, while you're at it.
EGG-COOKING METHOD

④ Now, let the dressing rain down! If you want something light and fresh, go with

_____ ; if you're looking for something creamy and
DRESSING THAT'LL MAKE YOU BOP AROUND

comforting, choose _____ .
DRESSING THAT'LL TUCK YOU INTO BED

⑤ Don't forget to garnish: wisps of _____ ,
FRUITS, VEGETABLES, PICKLES

_____ cheese, some _____ , and
TYPE OF CHEESE   FRESH HERBS

_____ . Finish with some sliced or smashed avocado—this is a
NUTS & SEEDS

grain bowl, after all.

HINTS AND WINKS

POPULAR WELLNESS PURSUIT
- yoga
- Pilates
- meditation
- spin class

TYPE OF GRAINS
- freekeh
- farro or wheat berries
- quinoa
- couscous
- polenta or grits
- leftover take-out rice

RAW VEGETABLES
- shaved carrots
- shredded Brussels sprouts
- slivered bell pepper
- handful of leafy greens

COOKED VEGETABLES
- roasted squash
- roasted or steamed cauliflower or broccoli
- braised or oil-poached mushrooms

COOKED PROTEIN
- canned tuna or salmon
- roasted or poached chicken
- sautéed shrimp
- bacon
- braised tempeh or tofu

EGG-COOKING METHOD
- poached
- fried
- soft- or hard-boiled
- pickled

DRESSING THAT'LL MAKE YOU BOP AROUND
- miso dressing
- balsamic vinaigrette
- chimichurri

DRESSING THAT'LL TUCK YOU INTO BED
- buttermilk ranch
- green goddess
- bacon vinaigrette
- blue cheese

FRUITS, VEGETABLES, PICKLES
- shaved or julienned apple
- persimmon or pear slices
- cucumber slices
- **Quick-Pickled Vegetables**

TYPE OF CHEESE
- ricotta
- blue
- goat
- feta
- Parmesan

FRESH HERBS
- dill
- basil
- chervil
- mint

NUTS & SEEDS
- almonds or walnuts
- sesame seeds
- furikake

QUICK-PICKLED VEGETABLES

Gather **1 pound assorted vegetables**—carrots, cucumbers, summer squash, radishes, jalapeños, cauliflower, and onions are surefire bets. Cut them into spears or slices and pack them into a big glass jar (since you're not doing this for long-term preservation, it doesn't have to be sterilized, but make sure it's squeaky clean). Make a brine with **1 cup water, 1 cup vinegar** (distilled white, cider, or rice), up to **¼ cup kosher salt,** up to **¼ cup sugar,** and any **whole spices** (bay leaves, sliced fresh ginger, red pepper flakes, mustard seeds) and **fresh herbs** (dill, oregano, cilantro) that are calling your name. If your veg are delicate enough for, say, a crudité platter, you can leave the brine cold; otherwise, bring it to an active simmer in a saucepan. Pour it directly into the jar, filling the jar all the way up to the top and making sure all the veg are submerged. Cover and refrigerate overnight for round-the-clock garnishing (and snacking).

NOTES TO YOUR FUTURE SELF

_____

_____

_____

_____

_____

BRAISED _____
BIG CENTERPIECE-Y CUT OF MEAT

WITH _____
ODDS & ENDS

---

① Preheat the oven to 375°F.

② In a large ovenproof pot or Dutch oven, let a few tablespoons of _____
COOKING FAT

get shimmery-hot over high heat. Rain some salt and pepper all over a 2½- to 5-pound

_____ , add it to the pot, and sear it well, a few minutes per side,
BIG CENTERPIECE-Y CUT OF MEAT

just to build a little color and crispiness on the outside.

③ Set the meat aside on a platter and drain all but a light coat of the remaining fat from the

pot. If you'd like, add some _____ to the pot and cook for a few
SAVORY TREATS

minutes; strain out and reserve the crispy bits.

④ Add some chopped _____ to the pot and stir, stir, stir to coat
STURDY VEGETABLES

with fat. Once they've softened a bit, add a couple teaspoons of _____
SPICES

or a couple tablespoons of _____ .
SOMETHING THICKER

⑤ When that starts smelling good, dribble in some _____ and use
FLAVORFUL LIQUID

your spoon to scrape up the browned bits from the bottom of the pan. Throw in a few

cups of _____ , chopped down to size if need be, and cook them
ODDS & ENDS

just enough to wake them up.

⑥ Return the meat to the pot and pour in some _____ , roughly
OTHER LIQUID

1 cup for every pound of meat. You won't regret a little swish of _____
SOMETHING PUNCHY

or a couple sprigs of _____ . Cover the pot, transfer it to the
FRESH HERBS

oven, and braise until the meat pulls off the bone. This can take just shy of 2 hours or

closer to 4 hours, so take up _____ while you wait patiently.
AN ACTIVITY THAT'LL KEEP YOU BUSY

⑦ Gently pull the meat out of the pot and set it off to the side. Return the pot to the stovetop

to let the sauce thicken. It's ready when it's somewhere between the consistency of a broth

and a gravy. Slice or shred the meat and spoon a mess of pan juices over it before serving.

HINTS AND WINKS

BIG CENTERPIECE-Y CUT OF MEAT
- pork shoulder
- whole chicken
- short ribs
- rump of beef
- lamb shanks

ODDS & ENDS
- mushrooms
- apples or oranges
- sweet potatoes
- winter squash
- olives
- sun-dried tomatoes

COOKING FAT
- olive or coconut oil
- butter or ghee
- schmaltz
- pork or bacon fat

SAVORY TREATS
- chopped bacon or pancetta
- anchovies

STURDY VEGETABLES
- red or yellow onions
- shallots
- leeks
- carrots
- celery

SPICES
- chili, five-spice, or curry powder
- ground coriander or cumin
- garam masala

SOMETHING THICKER
- tomato paste
- canned chipotles in adobo
- achiote paste

FLAVORFUL LIQUID
- stock
- wine or sherry
- tomato or pomegranate juice
- apple cider

OTHER LIQUID
- milk
- beer
- mole sauce

SOMETHING PUNCHY
- balsamic vinegar
- soy sauce
- fish sauce
- citrus zest or preserved lemons

FRESH HERBS
- thyme
- rosemary
- sage
- oregano
- parsley

AN ACTIVITY THAT'LL KEEP YOU BUSY
- knitting
- laundry
- pantry reorg

TIP

DON'T HAVE 4 HOURS TO SPARE?

If you're short on prep time, think small: use chicken leg quarters instead of a whole bird, or cut big pieces of meat like pork or lamb shoulder into more manageable 1½- to 2-inch pieces. (It's still a good idea to brown them in fat first.) You'll need less liquid, too—just enough to cradle the meat in a skillet with tall sides.

NOTES TO YOUR FUTURE SELF

_____

_____

_____

_____

_____

_____

BRASED _____
BIG CENTERPIECE-Y CUT OF MEAT

WITH _____
ODDS & ENDS

① Preheat the oven to 375°F.

② In a large ovenproof pot or Dutch oven, let a few tablespoons of _____
COOKING FAT

get shimmery-hot over high heat. Rain some salt and pepper all over a 2½- to 5-pound

_____ , add it to the pot, and sear it well, a few minutes per side,
BIG CENTERPIECE-Y CUT OF MEAT

just to build a little color and crispiness on the outside.

③ Set the meat aside on a platter and drain all but a light coat of the remaining fat from the

pot. If you'd like, add some _____ to the pot and cook for a few
SAVORY TREATS

minutes; strain out and reserve the crispy bits.

④ Add some chopped _____ to the pot and stir, stir, stir to coat
STURDY VEGETABLES

with fat. Once they've softened a bit, add a couple teaspoons of _____
SPICES

or a couple tablespoons of _____ .
SOMETHING THICKER

⑤ When that starts smelling good, dribble in some _____ and use
FLAVORFUL LIQUID

your spoon to scrape up the browned bits from the bottom of the pan. Throw in a few

cups of _____ , chopped down to size if need be, and cook them
ODDS & ENDS

just enough to wake them up.

⑥ Return the meat to the pot and pour in some _____ , roughly
OTHER LIQUID

1 cup for every pound of meat. You won't regret a little swish of _____
SOMETHING PUNCHY

or a couple sprigs of _____ . Cover the pot, transfer it to the
FRESH HERBS

oven, and braise until the meat pulls off the bone. This can take just shy of 2 hours or

closer to 4 hours, so take up _____ while you wait patiently.
AN ACTIVITY THAT'LL KEEP YOU BUSY

⑦ Gently pull the meat out of the pot and set it off to the side. Return the pot to the stovetop

to let the sauce thicken. It's ready when it's somewhere between the consistency of a broth

and a gravy. Slice or shred the meat and spoon a mess of pan juices over it before serving.

HINTS AND WINKS

BIG CENTERPIECE-Y CUT OF MEAT
- pork shoulder
- whole chicken
- short ribs
- rump of beef
- lamb shanks

ODDS & ENDS
- mushrooms
- apples or oranges
- sweet potatoes
- winter squash
- olives
- sun-dried tomatoes

COOKING FAT
- olive or coconut oil
- butter or ghee
- schmaltz
- pork or bacon fat

SAVORY TREATS
- chopped bacon or pancetta
- anchovies

STURDY VEGETABLES
- red or yellow onions
- shallots
- leeks
- carrots
- celery

SPICES
- chili, five-spice, or curry powder
- ground coriander or cumin
- garam masala

SOMETHING THICKER
- tomato paste
- canned chipotles in adobo
- achiote paste

FLAVORFUL LIQUID
- stock
- wine or sherry
- tomato or pomegranate juice
- apple cider

OTHER LIQUID
- milk
- beer
- mole sauce

SOMETHING PUNCHY
- balsamic vinegar
- soy sauce
- fish sauce
- citrus zest or preserved lemons

FRESH HERBS
- thyme
- rosemary
- sage
- oregano
- parsley

AN ACTIVITY THAT'LL KEEP YOU BUSY
- knitting
- laundry
- pantry reorg

TIP

DON'T HAVE 4 HOURS TO SPARE?

If you're short on prep time, think small: use chicken leg quarters instead of a whole bird, or cut big pieces of meat like pork or lamb shoulder into more manageable 1½- to 2-inch pieces. (It's still a good idea to brown them in fat first.) You'll need less liquid, too—just enough to cradle the meat in a skillet with tall sides.

NOTES TO YOUR FUTURE SELF

_____

_____

_____

_____

_____

BRAISED _____
BIG CENTERPIECE-Y CUT OF MEAT

WITH _____
ODDS & ENDS

① Preheat the oven to 375°F.

② In a large ovenproof pot or Dutch oven, let a few tablespoons of _____

COOKING FAT

get shimmery-hot over high heat. Rain some salt and pepper all over a 2½- to 5-pound

_____ , add it to the pot, and sear it well, a few minutes per side,

BIG CENTERPIECE-Y CUT OF MEAT

just to build a little color and crispiness on the outside.

③ Set the meat aside on a platter and drain all but a light coat of the remaining fat from the

pot. If you'd like, add some _____ to the pot and cook for a few

SAVORY TREATS

minutes; strain out and reserve the crispy bits.

④ Add some chopped _____ to the pot and stir, stir, stir to coat

STURDY VEGETABLES

with fat. Once they've softened a bit, add a couple teaspoons of _____

SPICES

or a couple tablespoons of _____ .

SOMETHING THICKER

⑤ When that starts smelling good, dribble in some _____ and use

FLAVORFUL LIQUID

your spoon to scrape up the browned bits from the bottom of the pan. Throw in a few

cups of _____ , chopped down to size if need be, and cook them

ODDS & ENDS

just enough to wake them up.

⑥ Return the meat to the pot and pour in some _____ , roughly

OTHER LIQUID

1 cup for every pound of meat. You won't regret a little swish of _____

SOMETHING PUNCHY

or a couple sprigs of _____ . Cover the pot, transfer it to the

FRESH HERBS

oven, and braise until the meat pulls off the bone. This can take just shy of 2 hours or

closer to 4 hours, so take up _____ while you wait patiently.

AN ACTIVITY THAT'LL KEEP YOU BUSY

⑦ Gently pull the meat out of the pot and set it off to the side. Return the pot to the stovetop

to let the sauce thicken. It's ready when it's somewhere between the consistency of a broth

and a gravy. Slice or shred the meat and spoon a mess of pan juices over it before serving.

HINTS AND WINKS

BIG CENTERPIECE-Y CUT OF MEAT
- pork shoulder
- whole chicken
- short ribs
- rump of beef
- lamb shanks

ODDS & ENDS
- mushrooms
- apples or oranges
- sweet potatoes
- winter squash
- olives
- sun-dried tomatoes

COOKING FAT
- olive or coconut oil
- butter or ghee
- schmaltz
- pork or bacon fat

SAVORY TREATS
- chopped bacon or pancetta
- anchovies

STURDY VEGETABLES
- red or yellow onions
- shallots
- leeks
- carrots
- celery

SPICES
- chili, five-spice, or curry powder
- ground coriander or cumin
- garam masala

SOMETHING THICKER
- tomato paste
- canned chipotles in adobo
- achiote paste

FLAVORFUL LIQUID
- stock
- wine or sherry
- tomato or pomegranate juice
- apple cider

OTHER LIQUID
- milk
- beer
- mole sauce

SOMETHING PUNCHY
- balsamic vinegar
- soy sauce
- fish sauce
- citrus zest or preserved lemons

FRESH HERBS
- thyme
- rosemary
- sage
- oregano
- parsley

AN ACTIVITY THAT'LL KEEP YOU BUSY
- knitting
- laundry
- pantry reorg

TIP

DON'T HAVE 4 HOURS TO SPARE?

If you're short on prep time, think small: use chicken leg quarters instead of a whole bird, or cut big pieces of meat like pork or lamb shoulder into more manageable 1½- to 2-inch pieces. (It's still a good idea to brown them in fat first.) You'll need less liquid, too—just enough to cradle the meat in a skillet with tall sides.

NOTES TO YOUR FUTURE SELF

_____

_____

_____

_____

_____

DEEP-DISH _____
PROTEIN OR MAIN EVENT
POTPIE

① Preheat the oven to 400°F.

② Chop a few stalks of celery and about a cup of _____ . For extra
ALLIUMS

coziness, add about 1 cup peeled and cubed _____ to your pile.
HEARTY VEGETABLES

③ Pour enough _____ into a large skillet to coat the bottom of the
COOKING FAT

pan and set the pan over medium heat. Add the celery and the alliums (and the hearty

vegetables, if you're using them) and let them sweat until they soften, about as long as it

takes to listen to _____ . Whisk in ¼ cup all-purpose flour and
YOUR FAVORITE SONG

cook for a couple of minutes.

④ Stir in 2 or so cups broth or stock, along with a large splash of _____ ,
SOMETHING CREAMY

salt, pepper, and maybe some _____ . Feeling adventurous?
SPICES

Add a glug of _____ and/or _____
FLAVORFUL BOOZE   FLAVORFUL SAUCE

sauce. Bump up the heat to high and bring it all to a boil, just until it thickens a bit.

⑤ Pull the pan off the heat. You're in the home stretch! Coax a few heaps of chopped

_____ into the mix, if you'd like. Once they've melded
HEARTY GREENS

with everything else, add some cooked _____ , chopped
PROTEIN OR MAIN EVENT

_____ , and minced _____ .
FRIENDLY VEGETABLES   FRESH HERBS

⑥ Pour the filling into a _____ and top it with
DEEP, COZY VESSEL

_____ . Pinch any edges to seal the roof and cut a few
A ROOF THAT'LL GET CRUSTY & GOLDEN

slits in it to let steam escape. Bake for 35 to 45 minutes, until the roof is golden brown

(tent the potpie with a swath of foil if it's browning too fast).

⑦ Summon all your willpower and let the potpie cool its jets for at least 15 minutes.

Don your snuggliest _____ and dig in.
SOFT ACCESSORY

HINTS AND WINKS

PROTEIN OR MAIN EVENT
- chicken
- beef
- mushroom
- lentil

ALLIUMS
- yellow or red onions
- shallots
- scallions
- leeks
- garlic

HEARTY VEGETABLES
- potatoes
- winter squash
- parsnips

COOKING FAT
- butter
- olive or coconut oil
- bacon fat

YOUR FAVORITE SONG
- "I Got You Babe" by Sonny & Cher
- "You Can Call Me Al" by Paul Simon
- "I Wanna Dance with Somebody" by Whitney Houston

SOMETHING CREAMY
- heavy cream
- half-and-half
- coconut milk

SPICES
- paprika
- grated nutmeg
- ground cumin
- curry powder
- celery salt

FLAVORFUL BOOZE
- white or red wine
- Madeira, sherry, or dry vermouth

FLAVORFUL SAUCE
- Worcestershire
- soy
- fish

HEARTY GREENS
- kale
- Swiss chard
- turnip or mustard greens

FRIENDLY VEGETABLES
- peas
- corn
- mushrooms
- green beans
- broccoli or cauliflower

FRESH HERBS
- parsley
- thyme
- basil
- oregano

DEEP, COZY VESSEL
- deep-dish pie plate
- 10-inch cast-iron skillet
- square/round casserole dish

A ROOF THAT'LL GET CRUSTY & GOLDEN
- **Pie Crust in a Pinch**
- puff pastry
- poufs of biscuit dough

SOFT ACCESSORY
- socks
- robe
- flannel
- earmuffs

WHIP IT UP

PIE CRUST IN A PINCH

Get ½ **cup (1 stick) butter** good and cold, ideally in the freezer. Break it down into small pieces, either by cutting it into little cubes or grating it on the coarsest holes of a box grater. If it softens, chill it again! You won't regret it. Separately, whisk a generous pinch of **salt** into **1 cup all-purpose flour**. Work the butter into the flour just enough for it to mingle and blend. Trickle in **1 tablespoon ice water** at a time, stirring between additions, until all the flour is just barely moistened. Dump the dough onto a floured counter and pat it into a disk. Swaddle it in plastic wrap and chill until firm. When you're ready to roll it out, scatter flour over your work surface, the dough, and your rolling pin, then roll it into a circle a little less than ¼-inch thick and a couple inches wider than your baking vessel.

NOTES TO YOUR FUTURE SELF

_____

_____

_____

_____

DEEP-DISH _____
PROTEIN OR MAIN EVENT
POTPIE

① Preheat the oven to 400°F.

② Chop a few stalks of celery and about a cup of _____ . For extra
ALLIUMS

coziness, add about 1 cup peeled and cubed _____ to your pile.
HEARTY VEGETABLES

③ Pour enough _____ into a large skillet to coat the bottom of the
COOKING FAT

pan and set the pan over medium heat. Add the celery and the alliums (and the hearty

vegetables, if you're using them) and let them sweat until they soften, about as long as it

takes to listen to _____ . Whisk in ¼ cup all-purpose flour and
YOUR FAVORITE SONG

cook for a couple of minutes.

④ Stir in 2 or so cups broth or stock, along with a large splash of _____ ,
SOMETHING CREAMY

salt, pepper, and maybe some _____ . Feeling adventurous?
SPICES

Add a glug of _____ and/or _____
FLAVORFUL BOOZE   FLAVORFUL SAUCE

sauce. Bump up the heat to high and bring it all to a boil, just until it thickens a bit.

⑤ Pull the pan off the heat. You're in the home stretch! Coax a few heaps of chopped

_____ into the mix, if you'd like. Once they've melded
HEARTY GREENS

with everything else, add some cooked _____ , chopped
PROTEIN OR MAIN EVENT

_____ , and minced _____ .
FRIENDLY VEGETABLES   FRESH HERBS

⑥ Pour the filling into a _____ and top it with
DEEP, COZY VESSEL

_____ . Pinch any edges to seal the roof and cut a few
A ROOF THAT'LL GET CRUSTY & GOLDEN

slits in it to let steam escape. Bake for 35 to 45 minutes, until the roof is golden brown

(tent the potpie with a swath of foil if it's browning too fast).

⑦ Summon all your willpower and let the potpie cool its jets for at least 15 minutes.

Don your snuggliest _____ and dig in.
SOFT ACCESSORY

HINTS AND WINKS

PROTEIN OR MAIN EVENT
- chicken
- beef
- mushroom
- lentil

ALLIUMS
- yellow or red onions
- shallots
- scallions
- leeks
- garlic

HEARTY VEGETABLES
- potatoes
- winter squash
- parsnips

COOKING FAT
- butter
- olive or coconut oil
- bacon fat

YOUR FAVORITE SONG
- "I Got You Babe" by Sonny & Cher
- "You Can Call Me Al" by Paul Simon
- "I Wanna Dance with Somebody" by Whitney Houston

SOMETHING CREAMY
- heavy cream
- half-and-half
- coconut milk

SPICES
- paprika
- grated nutmeg
- ground cumin
- curry powder
- celery salt

FLAVORFUL BOOZE
- white or red wine
- Madeira, sherry, or dry vermouth

FLAVORFUL SAUCE
- Worcestershire
- soy
- fish

HEARTY GREENS
- kale
- Swiss chard
- turnip or mustard greens

FRIENDLY VEGETABLES
- peas
- corn
- mushrooms
- green beans
- broccoli or cauliflower

FRESH HERBS
- parsley
- thyme
- basil
- oregano

DEEP, COZY VESSEL
- deep-dish pie plate
- 10-inch cast-iron skillet
- square/round casserole dish

A ROOF THAT'LL GET CRUSTY & GOLDEN
- **Pie Crust in a Pinch**
- puff pastry
- poufs of biscuit dough

SOFT ACCESSORY
- socks
- robe
- flannel
- earmuffs

PIE CRUST IN A PINCH

Get ½ **cup (1 stick) butter** good and cold, ideally in the freezer. Break it down into small pieces, either by cutting it into little cubes or grating it on the coarsest holes of a box grater. If it softens, chill it again! You won't regret it. Separately, whisk a generous pinch of **salt** into **1 cup all-purpose flour**. Work the butter into the flour just enough for it to mingle and blend. Trickle in **1 tablespoon ice water** at a time, stirring between additions, until all the flour is just barely moistened. Dump the dough onto a floured counter and pat it into a disk. Swaddle it in plastic wrap and chill until firm. When you're ready to roll it out, scatter flour over your work surface, the dough, and your rolling pin, then roll it into a circle a little less than ¼-inch thick and a couple inches wider than your baking vessel.

NOTES TO YOUR FUTURE SELF

_____

_____

_____

_____

DEEP-DISH _____
PROTEIN OR MAIN EVENT

POTPIE

① Preheat the oven to 400°F.

② Chop a few stalks of celery and about a cup of _____ . For extra
ALLIUMS

coziness, add about 1 cup peeled and cubed _____ to your pile.
HEARTY VEGETABLES

③ Pour enough _____ into a large skillet to coat the bottom of the
COOKING FAT

pan and set the pan over medium heat. Add the celery and the alliums (and the hearty

vegetables, if you're using them) and let them sweat until they soften, about as long as it

takes to listen to _____ . Whisk in ¼ cup all-purpose flour and
YOUR FAVORITE SONG

cook for a couple of minutes.

④ Stir in 2 or so cups broth or stock, along with a large splash of _____ ,
SOMETHING CREAMY

salt, pepper, and maybe some _____ . Feeling adventurous?
SPICES

Add a glug of _____ and/or _____
FLAVORFUL BOOZE   FLAVORFUL SAUCE

sauce. Bump up the heat to high and bring it all to a boil, just until it thickens a bit.

⑤ Pull the pan off the heat. You're in the home stretch! Coax a few heaps of chopped

_____ into the mix, if you'd like. Once they've melded
HEARTY GREENS

with everything else, add some cooked _____ , chopped
PROTEIN OR MAIN EVENT

_____ , and minced _____ .
FRIENDLY VEGETABLES   FRESH HERBS

⑥ Pour the filling into a _____ and top it with
DEEP, COZY VESSEL

_____ . Pinch any edges to seal the roof and cut a few
A ROOF THAT'LL GET CRUSTY & GOLDEN

slits in it to let steam escape. Bake for 35 to 45 minutes, until the roof is golden brown

(tent the potpie with a swath of foil if it's browning too fast).

⑦ Summon all your willpower and let the potpie cool its jets for at least 15 minutes.

Don your snuggliest _____ and dig in.
SOFT ACCESSORY

HINTS AND WINKS

PROTEIN OR MAIN EVENT
- chicken
- beef
- mushroom
- lentil

ALLIUMS
- yellow or red onions
- shallots
- scallions
- leeks
- garlic

HEARTY VEGETABLES
- potatoes
- winter squash
- parsnips

COOKING FAT
- butter
- olive or coconut oil
- bacon fat

YOUR FAVORITE SONG
- "I Got You Babe" by Sonny & Cher
- "You Can Call Me Al" by Paul Simon
- "I Wanna Dance with Somebody" by Whitney Houston

SOMETHING CREAMY
- heavy cream
- half-and-half
- coconut milk

SPICES
- paprika
- grated nutmeg
- ground cumin
- curry powder
- celery salt

FLAVORFUL BOOZE
- white or red wine
- Madeira, sherry, or dry vermouth

FLAVORFUL SAUCE
- Worcestershire
- soy
- fish

HEARTY GREENS
- kale
- Swiss chard
- turnip or mustard greens

FRIENDLY VEGETABLES
- peas
- corn
- mushrooms
- green beans
- broccoli or cauliflower

FRESH HERBS
- parsley
- thyme
- basil
- oregano

DEEP, COZY VESSEL
- deep-dish pie plate
- 10-inch cast-iron skillet
- square/round casserole dish

A ROOF THAT'LL GET CRUSTY & GOLDEN
- **Pie Crust in a Pinch**
- puff pastry
- poufs of biscuit dough

SOFT ACCESSORY
- socks
- robe
- flannel
- earmuffs

WHIP IT UP

PIE CRUST IN A PINCH

Get ½ cup (1 stick) butter good and cold, ideally in the freezer. Break it down into small pieces, either by cutting it into little cubes or grating it on the coarsest holes of a box grater. If it softens, chill it again! You won't regret it. Separately, whisk a generous pinch of **salt** into **1 cup all-purpose flour**. Work the butter into the flour just enough for it to mingle and blend. Trickle in **1 tablespoon ice water** at a time, stirring between additions, until all the flour is just barely moistened. Dump the dough onto a floured counter and pat it into a disk. Swaddle it in plastic wrap and chill until firm. When you're ready to roll it out, scatter flour over your work surface, the dough, and your rolling pin, then roll it into a circle a little less than ¼-inch thick and a couple inches wider than your baking vessel.

NOTES TO YOUR FUTURE SELF

_____

_____

_____

_____

FAMOUS _____
TYPE OF BEAN

BEAN CHILI

① Coat the bottom of a big stockpot with _____ and set it over
COOKING FAT

medium heat. Add about 1 cup diced onions, 1 cup diced _____ ,
VEGETABLES IN YOUR CRISPER

a diced _____ pepper or two, plus minced garlic, if you have it,
TYPE OF PEPPER

and season the vegetables with salt. Cook, stirring, until softened.

② Add a smattering of _____ , followed by two or three times that
NON-CHILI SPICES

amount of assorted ground chiles and/or chili powders (because: this is chili!).

③ Pour in 1 to 2 cans _____ tomatoes, a couple cans of
YOUR FAVORITE TYPE OF CANNED TOMATO

_____ beans (drained and rinsed), and about a can's worth of
TYPE OF BEAN

_____ . If you're looking for a protein boost, add
LIQUID

_____ now.
BONUS PROTEIN

④ Half cover your pot with a lid (like the pot's winking at you!) and simmer for about an

hour, until most of the liquid has evaporated, leaving behind a thick, rib-sticking stew. You

can use your spoon to coarsely mash the vegetables until they're the way you want them.

⑤ Add more spices as needed, then eat: over a scoop of _____ ,
COOKED GRAINS/MUSH

wrapped in or plopped on a _____ , or just straight up with a
BREADY PRODUCT

_____ .
UTENSIL

HINTS AND WINKS

TYPE OF BEAN
- kidney
- black
- white
- pinto

COOKING FAT
- olive, canola, or coconut oil
- butter
- pork or bacon fat

VEGETABLES IN YOUR CRISPER
- celery
- carrots
- leeks

TYPE OF PEPPER
- any combination of bell (red! green! yellow!) and hot (jalapeño, serrano, bird's-eye)

NON-CHILI SPICES
- ground cumin, coriander, or turmeric
- smoked paprika
- dried oregano

YOUR FAVORITE TYPE OF CANNED TOMATO
- diced
- fire-roasted
- chopped San Marzano

LIQUID
- water
- stock (vegetable, chicken, or beef)

BONUS PROTEIN
- chopped fresh or thawed frozen tofu
- tempeh
- cooked ground meat

COOKED GRAINS/MUSH
- rice
- farro
- polenta
- orzo

BREADY PRODUCT
- flour tortilla
- bun of sorts
- fleet of chips

UTENSIL
- spoon
- fork
- spork

TIP

GOT LEFTOVERS?

Stir any extra chili into your favorite **macaroni and cheese,** pile it onto **french fries** and top with cheese, or make it into a **chili burrito** creation with avocado, shredded lettuce, and (yep, you guessed it) cheese.

NOTES TO YOUR FUTURE SELF

FAMOUS _____
TYPE OF BEAN

BEAN CHILI

① Coat the bottom of a big stockpot with _____ and set it over
COOKING FAT

medium heat. Add about 1 cup diced onions, 1 cup diced _____ ,
VEGETABLES IN YOUR CRISPER

a diced _____ pepper or two, plus minced garlic, if you have it,
TYPE OF PEPPER

and season the vegetables with salt. Cook, stirring, until softened.

② Add a smattering of _____ , followed by two or three times that
NON-CHILI SPICES

amount of assorted ground chiles and/or chili powders (because: this is chili!).

③ Pour in 1 to 2 cans _____ tomatoes, a couple cans of
YOUR FAVORITE TYPE OF CANNED TOMATO

_____ beans (drained and rinsed), and about a can's worth of
TYPE OF BEAN

_____ . If you're looking for a protein boost, add
LIQUID

_____ now.
BONUS PROTEIN

④ Half cover your pot with a lid (like the pot's winking at you!) and simmer for about an

hour, until most of the liquid has evaporated, leaving behind a thick, rib-sticking stew. You

can use your spoon to coarsely mash the vegetables until they're the way you want them.

⑤ Add more spices as needed, then eat: over a scoop of _____ ,
COOKED GRAINS/MUSH

wrapped in or plopped on a _____ , or just straight up with a
BREADY PRODUCT

_____ .
UTENSIL

HINTS AND WINKS

TYPE OF BEAN
- kidney
- black
- white
- pinto

COOKING FAT
- olive, canola, or coconut oil
- butter
- pork or bacon fat

VEGETABLES IN YOUR CRISPER
- celery
- carrots
- leeks

TYPE OF PEPPER
- any combination of bell (red! green! yellow!) and hot (jalapeño, serrano, bird's-eye)

NON-CHILI SPICES
- ground cumin, coriander, or turmeric
- smoked paprika
- dried oregano

YOUR FAVORITE TYPE OF CANNED TOMATO
- diced
- fire-roasted
- chopped San Marzano

LIQUID
- water
- stock (vegetable, chicken, or beef)

BONUS PROTEIN
- chopped fresh or thawed frozen tofu
- tempeh
- cooked ground meat

COOKED GRAINS/MUSH
- rice
- farro
- polenta
- orzo

BREADY PRODUCT
- flour tortilla
- bun of sorts
- fleet of chips

UTENSIL
- spoon
- fork
- spork

TIP

GOT LEFTOVERS?

Stir any extra chili into your favorite **macaroni and cheese,** pile it onto **french fries** and top with cheese, or make it into a **chili burrito** creation with avocado, shredded lettuce, and (yep, you guessed it) cheese.

NOTES TO YOUR FUTURE SELF

_____

_____

_____

_____

_____

_____

FAMOUS _____
TYPE OF BEAN

BEAN CHILI

① Coat the bottom of a big stockpot with _____ and set it over
COOKING FAT

medium heat. Add about 1 cup diced onions, 1 cup diced _____ ,
VEGETABLES IN YOUR CRISPER

a diced _____ pepper or two, plus minced garlic, if you have it,
TYPE OF PEPPER

and season the vegetables with salt. Cook, stirring, until softened.

② Add a smattering of _____ , followed by two or three times that
NON-CHILI SPICES

amount of assorted ground chiles and/or chili powders (because: this is chili!).

③ Pour in 1 to 2 cans _____ tomatoes, a couple cans of
YOUR FAVORITE TYPE OF CANNED TOMATO

_____ beans (drained and rinsed), and about a can's worth of
TYPE OF BEAN

_____ . If you're looking for a protein boost, add
LIQUID

_____ now.
BONUS PROTEIN

④ Half cover your pot with a lid (like the pot's winking at you!) and simmer for about an

hour, until most of the liquid has evaporated, leaving behind a thick, rib-sticking stew. You

can use your spoon to coarsely mash the vegetables until they're the way you want them.

⑤ Add more spices as needed, then eat: over a scoop of _____ ,
COOKED GRAINS/MUSH

wrapped in or plopped on a _____ , or just straight up with a
BREADY PRODUCT

_____ .
UTENSIL

HINTS AND WINKS

TYPE OF BEAN
- kidney
- black
- white
- pinto

COOKING FAT
- olive, canola, or coconut oil
- butter
- pork or bacon fat

VEGETABLES IN YOUR CRISPER
- celery
- carrots
- leeks

TYPE OF PEPPER
- any combination of bell (red! green! yellow!) and hot (jalapeño, serrano, bird's-eye)

NON-CHILI SPICES
- ground cumin, coriander, or turmeric
- smoked paprika
- dried oregano

YOUR FAVORITE TYPE OF CANNED TOMATO
- diced
- fire-roasted
- chopped San Marzano

LIQUID
- water
- stock (vegetable, chicken, or beef)

BONUS PROTEIN
- chopped fresh or thawed frozen tofu
- tempeh
- cooked ground meat

COOKED GRAINS/MUSH
- rice
- farro
- polenta
- orzo

BREADY PRODUCT
- flour tortilla
- bun of sorts
- fleet of chips

UTENSIL
- spoon
- fork
- spork

TIP

GOT LEFTOVERS?

Stir any extra chili into your favorite **macaroni and cheese,** pile it onto **french fries** and top with cheese, or make it into a **chili burrito** creation with avocado, shredded lettuce, and (yep, you guessed it) cheese.

NOTES TO YOUR FUTURE SELF

_____

_____

_____

_____

_____

_____

ALLURING VEGETABLES

& _____ CHEESE

TYPE OF CHEESE

FRITTATA

① Preheat the oven to 400°F.

② In a large bowl, whisk 8 to 12 eggs with a few glugs of _____ .
SOMETHING CREAMY

Salt assertively and add some _____ and minced
SEASONING

_____ .
FRESH HERBS

③ Heat a few tablespoons of _____ in a large ovenproof skillet
COOKING FAT

over medium heat. If you're frying up any _____ , chop that and
MEAT

cook it first. When it's done, strain it out and set it off to the side.

④ Rally a few cups of chopped _____ and cook them right in the
ALLURING VEGETABLES

same skillet, on the stovetop or in the oven. Give sturdy ones—carrots, potatoes, winter

squash, etc.—a head start, since they'll take longer to cook. When they're partly cooked,

add tender vegetables like mushrooms.

⑤ Fold in a cup or so of grated or crumbled _____ cheese, plus the
TYPE OF CHEESE

cooked meat from earlier and maybe a couple handfuls of _____ .
OTHER MEAT

If you have cooked potatoes, sweet potatoes, or pasta, they'll be right at home here, too!

⑥ Pour the egg mixture into the skillet and bump the heat up to high, just for 30 seconds

or so. Sprinkle with another mound of _____ cheese, then
TYPE OF CHEESE

transfer to the oven and bake for 15 to 30 minutes, until the center is just barely set.

⑦ Remove the frittata from the oven and let it hang tight while you toss a simple salad.

Serve warm, at room temperature, or straight out of the fridge, cheered up with a hit

of balsamic vinegar or a squeeze of fresh lemon juice.

HINTS AND WINKS

ALLURING VEGETABLES
- onions or leeks
- garlic
- broccoli
- Brussels sprouts
- mushrooms
- any leftovers roaming your fridge

TYPE OF CHEESE
- Parmesan or pecorino
- cheddar
- Gruyère
- fontina
- Brie
- goat
- blue
- mozzarella
- feta

SOMETHING CREAMY
- cream
- milk
- yogurt
- crème fraîche
- coconut milk

SEASONING
- ground cumin, fennel, or coriander
- garam masala
- curry or chili powder
- red pepper flakes
- grated nutmeg
- soy sauce
- Dijon mustard

FRESH HERBS
- thyme
- sage
- oregano
- rosemary
- basil
- dill

COOKING FAT
- butter
- olive or coconut oil
- schmaltz
- pork or bacon fat

MEAT
- bacon
- pancetta
- sausage

OTHER MEAT
- sliced salami or ham
- shredded cooked chicken or pork

TIP

QUICHE-IFY THAT FRITTATA

Quiche is just a French word for "custardy frittata." Give yours the same laissez-faire attitude, and everyone wins. Start with the crust (there's a quick one in our potpie recipe), which you'll prebake in a pie plate and let cool. For the filling, you need only **3 eggs** and **1½ cups dairy**. Go wild with **cheese** and **seasoning** (maybe even save some to use as a topping!), but keep the bulkier add-ins, like **meat** and **vegetables,** to 2 cups max. Bake at 350°F until the edges are set but the middle is still a little wobbly, about 30 minutes, and let cool before serving.

NOTES TO YOUR FUTURE SELF

_____

_____

_____

_____

_____

_____

ALLURING VEGETABLES

& _____ CHEESE

TYPE OF CHEESE

FRITTATA

1. Preheat the oven to 400°F.

2. In a large bowl, whisk 8 to 12 eggs with a few glugs of _____.
   SOMETHING CREAMY

   Salt assertively and add some _____ and minced
   SEASONING

   _____ .
   FRESH HERBS

3. Heat a few tablespoons of _____ in a large ovenproof skillet
   COOKING FAT

   over medium heat. If you're frying up any _____ , chop that and
   MEAT

   cook it first. When it's done, strain it out and set it off to the side.

4. Rally a few cups of chopped _____ and cook them right in the
   ALLURING VEGETABLES

   same skillet, on the stovetop or in the oven. Give sturdy ones—carrots, potatoes, winter

   squash, etc.—a head start, since they'll take longer to cook. When they're partly cooked,

   add tender vegetables like mushrooms.

5. Fold in a cup or so of grated or crumbled _____ cheese, plus the
   TYPE OF CHEESE

   cooked meat from earlier and maybe a couple handfuls of _____ .
   OTHER MEAT

   If you have cooked potatoes, sweet potatoes, or pasta, they'll be right at home here, too!

6. Pour the egg mixture into the skillet and bump the heat up to high, just for 30 seconds

   or so. Sprinkle with another mound of _____ cheese, then
   TYPE OF CHEESE

   transfer to the oven and bake for 15 to 30 minutes, until the center is just barely set.

7. Remove the frittata from the oven and let it hang tight while you toss a simple salad.

   Serve warm, at room temperature, or straight out of the fridge, cheered up with a hit

   of balsamic vinegar or a squeeze of fresh lemon juice.

HINTS AND WINKS

ALLURING VEGETABLES
- onions or leeks
- garlic
- broccoli
- Brussels sprouts
- mushrooms
- any leftovers roaming your fridge

TYPE OF CHEESE
- Parmesan or pecorino
- cheddar
- Gruyère
- fontina
- Brie
- goat
- blue
- mozzarella
- feta

SOMETHING CREAMY
- cream
- milk
- yogurt
- crème fraîche
- coconut milk

SEASONING
- ground cumin, fennel, or coriander
- garam masala
- curry or chili powder
- red pepper flakes
- grated nutmeg
- soy sauce
- Dijon mustard

FRESH HERBS
- thyme
- sage
- oregano
- rosemary
- basil
- dill

COOKING FAT
- butter
- olive or coconut oil
- schmaltz
- pork or bacon fat

MEAT
- bacon
- pancetta
- sausage

OTHER MEAT
- sliced salami or ham
- shredded cooked chicken or pork

TIP

QUICHE-IFY THAT FRITTATA

Quiche is just a French word for "custardy frittata." Give yours the same laissez-faire attitude, and everyone wins. Start with the crust (there's a quick one in our potpie recipe), which you'll prebake in a pie plate and let cool. For the filling, you need only **3 eggs** and **1½ cups dairy**. Go wild with **cheese** and **seasoning** (maybe even save some to use as a topping!), but keep the bulkier add-ins, like **meat** and **vegetables,** to 2 cups max. Bake at 350°F until the edges are set but the middle is still a little wobbly, about 30 minutes, and let cool before serving.

NOTES TO YOUR FUTURE SELF

_____

_____

_____

_____

_____

ALLURING VEGETABLES

& _____ CHEESE
   TYPE OF CHEESE

FRITTATA

① Preheat the oven to 400°F.

② In a large bowl, whisk 8 to 12 eggs with a few glugs of _____.
                                                          SOMETHING CREAMY

Salt assertively and add some _____ and minced
                               SEASONING

_____ .
   FRESH HERBS

③ Heat a few tablespoons of _____ in a large ovenproof skillet
                             COOKING FAT

over medium heat. If you're frying up any _____ , chop that and
                                            MEAT

cook it first. When it's done, strain it out and set it off to the side.

④ Rally a few cups of chopped _____ and cook them right in the
                               ALLURING VEGETABLES

same skillet, on the stovetop or in the oven. Give sturdy ones—carrots, potatoes, winter

squash, etc.—a head start, since they'll take longer to cook. When they're partly cooked,

add tender vegetables like mushrooms.

⑤ Fold in a cup or so of grated or crumbled _____ cheese, plus the
                                              TYPE OF CHEESE

cooked meat from earlier and maybe a couple handfuls of _____ .
                                                          OTHER MEAT

If you have cooked potatoes, sweet potatoes, or pasta, they'll be right at home here, too!

⑥ Pour the egg mixture into the skillet and bump the heat up to high, just for 30 seconds

or so. Sprinkle with another mound of _____ cheese, then
                                        TYPE OF CHEESE

transfer to the oven and bake for 15 to 30 minutes, until the center is just barely set.

⑦ Remove the frittata from the oven and let it hang tight while you toss a simple salad.

Serve warm, at room temperature, or straight out of the fridge, cheered up with a hit

of balsamic vinegar or a squeeze of fresh lemon juice.

HINTS AND WINKS

ALLURING VEGETABLES
- onions or leeks
- garlic
- broccoli
- Brussels sprouts
- mushrooms
- any leftovers roaming your fridge

TYPE OF CHEESE
- Parmesan or pecorino
- cheddar
- Gruyère
- fontina
- Brie
- goat
- blue
- mozzarella
- feta

SOMETHING CREAMY
- cream
- milk
- yogurt
- crème fraîche
- coconut milk

SEASONING
- ground cumin, fennel, or coriander
- garam masala
- curry or chili powder
- red pepper flakes
- grated nutmeg
- soy sauce
- Dijon mustard

FRESH HERBS
- thyme
- sage
- oregano
- rosemary
- basil
- dill

COOKING FAT
- butter
- olive or coconut oil
- schmaltz
- pork or bacon fat

MEAT
- bacon
- pancetta
- sausage

OTHER MEAT
- sliced salami or ham
- shredded cooked chicken or pork

TIP

QUICHE-IFY THAT FRITTATA

Quiche is just a French word for "custardy frittata." Give yours the same laissez-faire attitude, and everyone wins. Start with the crust (there's a quick one in our potpie recipe), which you'll prebake in a pie plate and let cool. For the filling, you need only **3 eggs** and **1½ cups dairy**. Go wild with **cheese** and **seasoning** (maybe even save some to use as a topping!), but keep the bulkier add-ins, like **meat** and **vegetables,** to 2 cups max. Bake at 350°F until the edges are set but the middle is still a little wobbly, about 30 minutes, and let cool before serving.

NOTES TO YOUR FUTURE SELF

_____

_____

_____

_____

_____

SAVORY _____ PORRIDGE
TYPE OF GRAINS

WITH _____ & _____
HEARTY GREENS   SHREDDED COOKED MEAT

① Heat a couple tablespoons of _____ in a large saucepan or
COOKING FAT

Dutch oven over medium heat. Add your _____ —sturdier ones
AROMATICS

like onions go in first, while the likes of garlic and ginger join as those trailblazers are

finishing up. If you're using _____ , add them to the pan and
SPICES

give a little stir till they start to open up and become fragrant.

② Mix in 1 cup _____ and toast for a couple of minutes. Add
TYPE OF GRAINS

_____ stock; use a 3:1 ratio of stock to grain(s) if you're short
TYPE OF STOCK

on time, but 6:1 (or even 8:1) is ideal for a porridge you can curl up with. Turn the heat

down to low. Start watching _____ and return to the pot every
YOUR FAVORITE OLD MOVIE

so often to coddle, nudge, and give pep talks. With time, the grains will start to break

down and melt into one another.

③ After almost all the stock has been absorbed, remove any whole aromatics, season with

salt and more spices, and stir in up to 2 cups each _____ and/or
HEARTY GREENS

_____ , which need time to mingle before the other guests arrive.
SHREDDED COOKED MEAT

④ When you've attained a sufficiently cushy porridge (depending on how much stock you've

added, this can take anywhere from 45 minutes to 2 hours), take the pot off the heat.

Fold in a few tablespoons of _____ —or just 1 to 2 teaspoons of something
SAUCE OR JUICE

more intense, like fish sauce or oyster sauce—plus a cup or so of grated or crumbled

_____ cheese, a heap of _____ , and up
TYPE OF CHEESE   COOKED VEGETABLES

to 2 cups _____ .
MORE COOKED PROTEIN

⑤ Ladle the porridge into a bowl that can be cradled in both palms. Top it off with a big

pinch of _____ , an enthusiastic spoonful of _____ ,
CRISPY BITS   FRESH OR BOLD GARNISH

and your choice of some **Soy-Sauced Eggs** or avocado slices. Jackson Pollock some

_____ all over, if you're into it. Nose-dive in.
LUXE SAUCE

HINTS AND WINKS

TYPE OF GRAINS
- white or brown rice
- rolled (not quick) oats
- farro
- quinoa
- barley

HEARTY GREENS
- kale
- Swiss chard
- turnip or beet greens

SHREDDED COOKED MEAT
- roast chicken
- pot roast or brisket
- anything braised

COOKING FAT
- butter or ghee
- olive or coconut oil

AROMATICS
- yellow onions
- leeks
- garlic
- ginger or lemongrass
- bay leaves
- fresh rosemary
- fresh sage

SPICES
- curry powder
- chili powder
- ground cumin or fennel
- five-spice powder

TYPE OF STOCK
- chicken
- vegetable
- mushroom

YOUR FAVORITE OLD MOVIE
- *10 Things I Hate About You*
- *Best in Show*
- *The Philadelphia Story*

SAUCE OR JUICE
- brown butter
- tahini
- tamari or soy sauce
- hot sauce
- heavy cream
- miso slurry

TYPE OF CHEESE
- Parmesan or pecorino
- Gouda
- goat

COOKED VEGETABLES
- mushrooms
- Brussels sprouts
- broccoli
- beets

MORE COOKED PROTEIN
- sausage
- meatballs
- fried tofu

CRISPY BITS
- toasted nuts or seeds
- fried shallots
- roasted seaweed

FRESH OR BOLD GARNISH
- chopped radish or fennel
- microgreens
- kimchi

LUXE SAUCE
- hollandaise
- pesto
- romesco
- Bolognese

WHIP IT UP

SOY-SAUCED EGGS

Hard-boil (or boil to your preferred doneness) **however many eggs you like,** let them cool, then peel them. In a small saucepan, combine **soy sauce, rice vinegar, brown sugar,** and **water**—for every 6 eggs, you'll want about 3 tablespoons soy sauce and 2 tablespoons vinegar, plus about 1 tablespoon each of sugar and water. Bring the mixture to a simmer over medium heat. Remove from the heat, then add the peeled eggs. Roll the eggs around in the sauce until they're coated and infused with flavor, 5 to 10 minutes. Remove with a slotted spoon. (These will keep for a couple days, refrigerated in an airtight container.)

NOTES TO YOUR FUTURE SELF

_____

_____

_____

_____

_____

SAVORY _____ PORRIDGE
TYPE OF GRAINS

WITH _____ & _____
HEARTY GREENS   SHREDDED COOKED MEAT

① Heat a couple tablespoons of _____ in a large saucepan or
COOKING FAT

Dutch oven over medium heat. Add your _____ —sturdier ones
AROMATICS

like onions go in first, while the likes of garlic and ginger join as those trailblazers are

finishing up. If you're using _____ , add them to the pan and
SPICES

give a little stir till they start to open up and become fragrant.

② Mix in 1 cup _____ and toast for a couple of minutes. Add
TYPE OF GRAINS

_____ stock; use a 3:1 ratio of stock to grain(s) if you're short
TYPE OF STOCK

on time, but 6:1 (or even 8:1) is ideal for a porridge you can curl up with. Turn the heat

down to low. Start watching _____ and return to the pot every
YOUR FAVORITE OLD MOVIE

so often to coddle, nudge, and give pep talks. With time, the grains will start to break

down and melt into one another.

③ After almost all the stock has been absorbed, remove any whole aromatics, season with

salt and more spices, and stir in up to 2 cups each _____ and/or
HEARTY GREENS

_____ , which need time to mingle before the other guests arrive.
SHREDDED COOKED MEAT

④ When you've attained a sufficiently cushy porridge (depending on how much stock you've

added, this can take anywhere from 45 minutes to 2 hours), take the pot off the heat.

Fold in a few tablespoons of _____ —or just 1 to 2 teaspoons of something
SAUCE OR JUICE

more intense, like fish sauce or oyster sauce—plus a cup or so of grated or crumbled

_____ cheese, a heap of _____ , and up
TYPE OF CHEESE   COOKED VEGETABLES

to 2 cups _____ .
MORE COOKED PROTEIN

⑤ Ladle the porridge into a bowl that can be cradled in both palms. Top it off with a big

pinch of _____ , an enthusiastic spoonful of _____ ,
CRISPY BITS   FRESH OR BOLD GARNISH

and your choice of some **Soy-Sauced Eggs** or avocado slices. Jackson Pollock some

_____ all over, if you're into it. Nose-dive in.
LUXE SAUCE

HINTS AND WINKS

TYPE OF GRAINS
- white or brown rice
- rolled (not quick) oats
- farro
- quinoa
- barley

HEARTY GREENS
- kale
- Swiss chard
- turnip or beet greens

SHREDDED COOKED MEAT
- roast chicken
- pot roast or brisket
- anything braised

COOKING FAT
- butter or ghee
- olive or coconut oil

AROMATICS
- yellow onions
- leeks
- garlic
- ginger or lemongrass
- bay leaves
- fresh rosemary
- fresh sage

SPICES
- curry powder
- chili powder
- ground cumin or fennel
- five-spice powder

TYPE OF STOCK
- chicken
- vegetable
- mushroom

YOUR FAVORITE OLD MOVIE
- *10 Things I Hate About You*
- *Best in Show*
- *The Philadelphia Story*

SAUCE OR JUICE
- brown butter
- tahini
- tamari or soy sauce
- hot sauce
- heavy cream
- miso slurry

TYPE OF CHEESE
- Parmesan or pecorino
- Gouda
- goat

COOKED VEGETABLES
- mushrooms
- Brussels sprouts
- broccoli
- beets

MORE COOKED PROTEIN
- sausage
- meatballs
- fried tofu

CRISPY BITS
- toasted nuts or seeds
- fried shallots
- roasted seaweed

FRESH OR BOLD GARNISH
- chopped radish or fennel
- microgreens
- kimchi

LUXE SAUCE
- hollandaise
- pesto
- romesco
- Bolognese

WHIP IT UP

SOY-SAUCED EGGS

Hard-boil (or boil to your preferred doneness) **however many eggs you like,** let them cool, then peel them. In a small saucepan, combine **soy sauce, rice vinegar, brown sugar,** and **water**—for every 6 eggs, you'll want about 3 tablespoons soy sauce and 2 tablespoons vinegar, plus about 1 tablespoon each of sugar and water. Bring the mixture to a simmer over medium heat. Remove from the heat, then add the peeled eggs. Roll the eggs around in the sauce until they're coated and infused with flavor, 5 to 10 minutes. Remove with a slotted spoon. (These will keep for a couple days, refrigerated in an airtight container.)

NOTES TO YOUR FUTURE SELF

_____

_____

_____

_____

SAVORY _____ PORRIDGE
TYPE OF GRAINS

WITH _____ & _____
HEARTY GREENS   SHREDDED COOKED MEAT

①   Heat a couple tablespoons of _____ in a large saucepan or
COOKING FAT

Dutch oven over medium heat. Add your _____ —sturdier ones
AROMATICS

like onions go in first, while the likes of garlic and ginger join as those trailblazers are

finishing up. If you're using _____ , add them to the pan and
SPICES

give a little stir till they start to open up and become fragrant.

②   Mix in 1 cup _____ and toast for a couple of minutes. Add
TYPE OF GRAINS

_____ stock; use a 3:1 ratio of stock to grain(s) if you're short
TYPE OF STOCK

on time, but 6:1 (or even 8:1) is ideal for a porridge you can curl up with. Turn the heat

down to low. Start watching _____ and return to the pot every
YOUR FAVORITE OLD MOVIE

so often to coddle, nudge, and give pep talks. With time, the grains will start to break

down and melt into one another.

③   After almost all the stock has been absorbed, remove any whole aromatics, season with

salt and more spices, and stir in up to 2 cups each _____ and/or
HEARTY GREENS

_____ , which need time to mingle before the other guests arrive.
SHREDDED COOKED MEAT

④   When you've attained a sufficiently cushy porridge (depending on how much stock you've

added, this can take anywhere from 45 minutes to 2 hours), take the pot off the heat.

Fold in a few tablespoons of _____ —or just 1 to 2 teaspoons of something
SAUCE OR JUICE

more intense, like fish sauce or oyster sauce—plus a cup or so of grated or crumbled

_____ cheese, a heap of _____ , and up
TYPE OF CHEESE   COOKED VEGETABLES

to 2 cups _____ .
MORE COOKED PROTEIN

⑤   Ladle the porridge into a bowl that can be cradled in both palms. Top it off with a big

pinch of _____ , an enthusiastic spoonful of _____ ,
CRISPY BITS   FRESH OR BOLD GARNISH

and your choice of some **Soy-Sauced Eggs** or avocado slices. Jackson Pollock some

_____ all over, if you're into it. Nose-dive in.
LUXE SAUCE

HINTS AND WINKS

TYPE OF GRAINS
- white or brown rice
- rolled (not quick) oats
- farro
- quinoa
- barley

HEARTY GREENS
- kale
- Swiss chard
- turnip or beet greens

SHREDDED COOKED MEAT
- roast chicken
- pot roast or brisket
- anything braised

COOKING FAT
- butter or ghee
- olive or coconut oil

AROMATICS
- yellow onions
- leeks
- garlic
- ginger or lemongrass
- bay leaves
- fresh rosemary
- fresh sage

SPICES
- curry powder
- chili powder
- ground cumin or fennel
- five-spice powder

TYPE OF STOCK
- chicken
- vegetable
- mushroom

YOUR FAVORITE OLD MOVIE
- *10 Things I Hate About You*
- *Best in Show*
- *The Philadelphia Story*

SAUCE OR JUICE
- brown butter
- tahini
- tamari or soy sauce
- hot sauce
- heavy cream
- miso slurry

TYPE OF CHEESE
- Parmesan or pecorino
- Gouda
- goat

COOKED VEGETABLES
- mushrooms
- Brussels sprouts
- broccoli
- beets

MORE COOKED PROTEIN
- sausage
- meatballs
- fried tofu

CRISPY BITS
- toasted nuts or seeds
- fried shallots
- roasted seaweed

FRESH OR BOLD GARNISH
- chopped radish or fennel
- microgreens
- kimchi

LUXE SAUCE
- hollandaise
- pesto
- romesco
- Bolognese

WHIP IT UP
SOY-SAUCED EGGS

Hard-boil (or boil to your preferred doneness) **however many eggs you like,** let them cool, then peel them. In a small saucepan, combine **soy sauce, rice vinegar, brown sugar,** and **water**—for every 6 eggs, you'll want about 3 tablespoons soy sauce and 2 tablespoons vinegar, plus about 1 tablespoon each of sugar and water. Bring the mixture to a simmer over medium heat. Remove from the heat, then add the peeled eggs. Roll the eggs around in the sauce until they're coated and infused with flavor, 5 to 10 minutes. Remove with a slotted spoon. (These will keep for a couple days, refrigerated in an airtight container.)

NOTES TO YOUR FUTURE SELF
_____

_____

_____

_____

_____

_____'s _____

YOUR NAME   SUPERLATIVE

GRILLED CHEESE

① For each sandwich, lay out two slices of _____ bread and spread

TYPE OF BREAD

a thin, even layer of mayo or softened butter over each one.

② Flip the bread. If you'd like, cover it with a little _____ or another

SPREAD

pat of butter.

③ Grate or slice some _____ cheese and pile one or two handfuls

MELTY CHEESE

on one piece of bread per sandwich, on the side that has the spread. Follow closely

behind with _____ , plus maybe a couple

ADD-INS THAT TUG AT YOUR HEARTSTRINGS

tablespoons of _____ cheese. Top with the other piece of

ACCENT CHEESE

bread, mayo'd/buttered side out.

④ Get a large skillet nice and toasty over medium-low heat. Drop in a sandwich and fry it

on each side for 4 to 5 minutes, until the bread is crispy and the insides are molten.

Repeat with the other sandwiches.

⑤ Slice the sandwiches diagonally. Eat them solo or dunked in **Tomato Soup**.

HINTS AND WINKS

SUPERLATIVE
- ooziest
- ultimate
- perfect

TYPE OF BREAD
- white
- wheat
- sourdough
- ciabatta
- whole grain
- brioche
- Hawaiian

SPREAD
- Dijon mustard
- pesto
- aioli
- pepper jelly
- good jam
- membrillo
- mostarda
- spicy honey

MELTY CHEESE
- cheddar
- American
- pepper Jack
- Gruyère
- mozzarella
- fontina
- Gouda
- Brie

ADD-INS THAT TUG AT YOUR HEARTSTRINGS
- sliced salami or prosciutto
- cooked bacon
- caramelized onions
- braised greens
- basil leaves
- arugula
- a fried egg
- chopped cornichons or olives

ACCENT CHEESE
- goat or pimiento
- feta
- pecorino

WHIP IT UP

TOMATO SOUP

Chop **1 or 2 onions**. In a large pot or Dutch oven, cook the onions in **oil or butter** with **salt** and a good pinch of any **spices and herbs** you'd like. Pour in a **28-ounce can of your favorite tomatoes** and crush them till they're where you want them. Bring to a simmer; cook to reduce if you want it thicker, or add a splash of **stock or water** to thin it out. Swirl in some **heavy cream** to finish if you're feeling flush. Purée with an immersion blender, or don't.

NOTES TO YOUR FUTURE SELF

_____

_____

_____

_____

_____

_____'s _____

YOUR NAME   SUPERLATIVE

GRILLED CHEESE

① For each sandwich, lay out two slices of _____ bread and spread

    TYPE OF BREAD

a thin, even layer of mayo or softened butter over each one.

② Flip the bread. If you'd like, cover it with a little _____ or another

    SPREAD

pat of butter.

③ Grate or slice some _____ cheese and pile one or two handfuls

    MELTY CHEESE

on one piece of bread per sandwich, on the side that has the spread. Follow closely

behind with _____ , plus maybe a couple

    ADD-INS THAT TUG AT YOUR HEARTSTRINGS

tablespoons of _____ cheese. Top with the other piece of

    ACCENT CHEESE

bread, mayo'd/buttered side out.

④ Get a large skillet nice and toasty over medium-low heat. Drop in a sandwich and fry it

on each side for 4 to 5 minutes, until the bread is crispy and the insides are molten.

Repeat with the other sandwiches.

⑤ Slice the sandwiches diagonally. Eat them solo or dunked in **Tomato Soup**.

HINTS AND WINKS

SUPERLATIVE
- ooziest
- ultimate
- perfect

TYPE OF BREAD
- white
- wheat
- sourdough
- ciabatta
- whole grain
- brioche
- Hawaiian

SPREAD
- Dijon mustard
- pesto
- aioli
- pepper jelly
- good jam
- membrillo
- mostarda
- spicy honey

MELTY CHEESE
- cheddar
- American
- pepper Jack
- Gruyère
- mozzarella
- fontina
- Gouda
- Brie

ADD-INS THAT TUG AT YOUR HEARTSTRINGS
- sliced salami or prosciutto
- cooked bacon
- caramelized onions
- braised greens
- basil leaves
- arugula
- a fried egg
- chopped cornichons or olives

ACCENT CHEESE
- goat or pimiento
- feta
- pecorino

WHIP IT UP

TOMATO SOUP

Chop **1 or 2 onions**. In a large pot or Dutch oven, cook the onions in **oil or butter** with **salt** and a good pinch of any **spices and herbs** you'd like. Pour in a **28-ounce can of your favorite tomatoes** and crush them till they're where you want them. Bring to a simmer; cook to reduce if you want it thicker, or add a splash of **stock or water** to thin it out. Swirl in some **heavy cream** to finish if you're feeling flush. Purée with an immersion blender, or don't.

NOTES TO YOUR FUTURE SELF

_____ 'S _____
        YOUR NAME   SUPERLATIVE

GRILLED CHEESE

① For each sandwich, lay out two slices of _____ bread and spread
                                                    TYPE OF BREAD

a thin, even layer of mayo or softened butter over each one.

② Flip the bread. If you'd like, cover it with a little _____ or another
                                                                SPREAD

pat of butter.

③ Grate or slice some _____ cheese and pile one or two handfuls
                                MELTY CHEESE

on one piece of bread per sandwich, on the side that has the spread. Follow closely

behind with _____ , plus maybe a couple
                ADD-INS THAT TUG AT YOUR HEARTSTRINGS

tablespoons of _____ cheese. Top with the other piece of
                        ACCENT CHEESE

bread, mayo'd/buttered side out.

④ Get a large skillet nice and toasty over medium-low heat. Drop in a sandwich and fry it

on each side for 4 to 5 minutes, until the bread is crispy and the insides are molten.

Repeat with the other sandwiches.

⑤ Slice the sandwiches diagonally. Eat them solo or dunked in **Tomato Soup**.

HINTS AND WINKS

SUPERLATIVE
- ooziest
- ultimate
- perfect

TYPE OF BREAD
- white
- wheat
- sourdough
- ciabatta
- whole grain
- brioche
- Hawaiian

SPREAD
- Dijon mustard
- pesto
- aioli
- pepper jelly
- good jam
- membrillo
- mostarda
- spicy honey

MELTY CHEESE
- cheddar
- American
- pepper Jack
- Gruyère
- mozzarella
- fontina
- Gouda
- Brie

ADD-INS THAT TUG AT YOUR HEARTSTRINGS
- sliced salami or prosciutto
- cooked bacon
- caramelized onions
- braised greens
- basil leaves
- arugula
- a fried egg
- chopped cornichons or olives

ACCENT CHEESE
- goat or pimiento
- feta
- pecorino

TOMATO SOUP

Chop **1 or 2 onions**. In a large pot or Dutch oven, cook the onions in **oil or butter** with **salt** and a good pinch of any **spices and herbs** you'd like. Pour in a **28-ounce can of your favorite tomatoes** and crush them till they're where you want them. Bring to a simmer; cook to reduce if you want it thicker, or add a splash of **stock or water** to thin it out. Swirl in some **heavy cream** to finish if you're feeling flush. Purée with an immersion blender, or don't.

NOTES TO YOUR FUTURE SELF

_____

_____

_____

_____

_____

_____

ADJECTIVE TO DESCRIBE GOOD FOOD

LENTIL SOUP

① Sort and rinse your _____ lentils. (This step may seem optional,
TYPE OF LENTIL

but it's necessary so you can catch any tiny stones or other non-lentil bits.)

② Heat a glug or two of olive oil in a big soup pot over medium heat. Add about 1 cup

diced _____ and a couple of smashed garlic cloves.
AROMATICS

Give it all a stir with a big wooden spoon. Cook, stirring occasionally, until soft and

fragrant, then throw in a cup or two of chopped _____ and
VEG OF ALL KINDS

_____ . (Don't forget salt and pepper!)
PANTRY/FRIDGE SPICES & HERBS

③ Add the lentils and _____ (4 or 5 cups for 1 cup lentils) and stir
COOKING LIQUID

everything together as if you're brewing a healing elixir. Bring to a boil over high heat,

then take the heat back down to medium-low and let it all cook, giving it a stir every now

and then, until the lentils are just tender (not mushy) and the vegetables are soft. (This

should take around 20 minutes for most kinds of lentils; a little less for red or yellow.)

④ Add a couple handfuls of chopped _____ . Cook until the
GREENS

greens are wilted—just a minute or two for delicate greens, and a few more minutes for

heartier ones—then give it a taste. What does it need? Add more salt, pepper, or spices to

round it out, then drizzle/sprinkle with _____ and dollop with
FINISHING TOUCH

_____ .
SOMETHING CREAMY

⑤ Ladle into bowls, top with _____ for textural contrast, and serve
SOMETHING CRUNCHY

with _____ for dunking.
SOMETHING BREADY

HINTS AND WINKS

ADJECTIVE TO DESCRIBE GOOD FOOD
- hearty
- warming
- rich

TYPE OF LENTIL
- French
- beluga
- black
- Le Puy
- red
- green
- yellow

AROMATICS
- onions
- carrots
- celery
- ginger or lemongrass
- scallions

VEG OF ALL KINDS
- bell peppers
- winter squash
- parsnips
- fennel
- sweet potato
- beets
- cauliflower

PANTRY/FRIDGE SPICES & HERBS
- lemon zest
- curry powder
- ground turmeric, cumin, or coriander
- smoked paprika
- bay leaves
- thyme
- rosemary

COOKING LIQUID
- stock (vegetable, chicken, or beef)
- coconut milk
- **Parmesan Broth**

GREENS
- kale
- collard greens
- beet greens
- spinach
- chard
- mustard greens
- watercress

FINISHING TOUCH
- olive oil
- sherry vinegar
- lemon juice
- sriracha
- harissa

SOMETHING CREAMY
- yogurt, crème fraîche, or sour cream
- tahini

SOMETHING CRUNCHY
- dukkah
- toasted nuts
- croutons
- oyster crackers

SOMETHING BREADY
- toast soldiers
- sliced focaccia
- grilled cheese toasts

PARMESAN BROTH

In a large pot, cover **leftover Parmesan rinds** with roughly 8 times their volume of **water**. Bring the mixture to a boil, then simmer it for an hour or two, until it's as flavorful as you like. Use immediately or let cool, then store in an airtight container in your fridge for up to 1 week or freeze for up to 3 months.

NOTES TO YOUR FUTURE SELF

ADJECTIVE TO DESCRIBE GOOD FOOD

LENTIL SOUP

① Sort and rinse your _____ lentils. (This step may seem optional,
TYPE OF LENTIL
but it's necessary so you can catch any tiny stones or other non-lentil bits.)

② Heat a glug or two of olive oil in a big soup pot over medium heat. Add about 1 cup

diced _____ and a couple of smashed garlic cloves.
AROMATICS
Give it all a stir with a big wooden spoon. Cook, stirring occasionally, until soft and

fragrant, then throw in a cup or two of chopped _____ and
VEG OF ALL KINDS
_____ . (Don't forget salt and pepper!)
PANTRY/FRIDGE SPICES & HERBS

③ Add the lentils and _____ (4 or 5 cups for 1 cup lentils) and stir
COOKING LIQUID
everything together as if you're brewing a healing elixir. Bring to a boil over high heat,

then take the heat back down to medium-low and let it all cook, giving it a stir every now

and then, until the lentils are just tender (not mushy) and the vegetables are soft. (This

should take around 20 minutes for most kinds of lentils; a little less for red or yellow.)

④ Add a couple handfuls of chopped _____ . Cook until the
GREENS
greens are wilted—just a minute or two for delicate greens, and a few more minutes for

heartier ones—then give it a taste. What does it need? Add more salt, pepper, or spices to

round it out, then drizzle/sprinkle with _____ and dollop with
FINISHING TOUCH
_____ .
SOMETHING CREAMY

⑤ Ladle into bowls, top with _____ for textural contrast, and serve
SOMETHING CRUNCHY
with _____ for dunking.
SOMETHING BREADY

HINTS AND WINKS

ADJECTIVE TO DESCRIBE GOOD FOOD
- hearty
- warming
- rich

TYPE OF LENTIL
- French
- beluga
- black
- Le Puy
- red
- green
- yellow

AROMATICS
- onions
- carrots
- celery
- ginger or lemongrass
- scallions

VEG OF ALL KINDS
- bell peppers
- winter squash
- parsnips
- fennel
- sweet potato
- beets
- cauliflower

PANTRY/FRIDGE SPICES & HERBS
- lemon zest
- curry powder
- ground turmeric, cumin, or coriander
- smoked paprika
- bay leaves
- thyme
- rosemary

COOKING LIQUID
- stock (vegetable, chicken, or beef)
- coconut milk
- **Parmesan Broth**

GREENS
- kale
- collard greens
- beet greens
- spinach
- chard
- mustard greens
- watercress

FINISHING TOUCH
- olive oil
- sherry vinegar
- lemon juice
- sriracha
- harissa

SOMETHING CREAMY
- yogurt, crème fraîche, or sour cream
- tahini

SOMETHING CRUNCHY
- dukkah
- toasted nuts
- croutons
- oyster crackers

SOMETHING BREADY
- toast soldiers
- sliced focaccia
- grilled cheese toasts

PARMESAN BROTH

In a large pot, cover **leftover Parmesan rinds** with roughly 8 times their volume of **water**. Bring the mixture to a boil, then simmer it for an hour or two, until it's as flavorful as you like. Use immediately or let cool, then store in an airtight container in your fridge for up to 1 week or freeze for up to 3 months.

NOTES TO YOUR FUTURE SELF

_____

_____

_____

_____

_____

ADJECTIVE TO DESCRIBE GOOD FOOD
LENTIL SOUP

① Sort and rinse your _____ lentils. (This step may seem optional,
TYPE OF LENTIL

but it's necessary so you can catch any tiny stones or other non-lentil bits.)

② Heat a glug or two of olive oil in a big soup pot over medium heat. Add about 1 cup

diced _____ and a couple of smashed garlic cloves.
AROMATICS

Give it all a stir with a big wooden spoon. Cook, stirring occasionally, until soft and

fragrant, then throw in a cup or two of chopped _____ and
VEG OF ALL KINDS

_____ . (Don't forget salt and pepper!)
PANTRY/FRIDGE SPICES & HERBS

③ Add the lentils and _____ (4 or 5 cups for 1 cup lentils) and stir
COOKING LIQUID

everything together as if you're brewing a healing elixir. Bring to a boil over high heat,

then take the heat back down to medium-low and let it all cook, giving it a stir every now

and then, until the lentils are just tender (not mushy) and the vegetables are soft. (This

should take around 20 minutes for most kinds of lentils; a little less for red or yellow.)

④ Add a couple handfuls of chopped _____ . Cook until the
GREENS

greens are wilted—just a minute or two for delicate greens, and a few more minutes for

heartier ones—then give it a taste. What does it need? Add more salt, pepper, or spices to

round it out, then drizzle/sprinkle with _____ and dollop with
FINISHING TOUCH

_____ .
SOMETHING CREAMY

⑤ Ladle into bowls, top with _____ for textural contrast, and serve
SOMETHING CRUNCHY

with _____ for dunking.
SOMETHING BREADY

HINTS AND WINKS

ADJECTIVE TO DESCRIBE GOOD FOOD
- hearty
- warming
- rich

TYPE OF LENTIL
- French
- beluga
- black
- Le Puy
- red
- green
- yellow

AROMATICS
- onions
- carrots
- celery
- ginger or lemongrass
- scallions

VEG OF ALL KINDS
- bell peppers
- winter squash
- parsnips
- fennel
- sweet potato
- beets
- cauliflower

PANTRY/FRIDGE SPICES & HERBS
- lemon zest
- curry powder
- ground turmeric, cumin, or coriander
- smoked paprika
- bay leaves
- thyme
- rosemary

COOKING LIQUID
- stock (vegetable, chicken, or beef)
- coconut milk
- **Parmesan Broth**

GREENS
- kale
- collard greens
- beet greens
- spinach
- chard
- mustard greens
- watercress

FINISHING TOUCH
- olive oil
- sherry vinegar
- lemon juice
- sriracha
- harissa

SOMETHING CREAMY
- yogurt, crème fraîche, or sour cream
- tahini

SOMETHING CRUNCHY
- dukkah
- toasted nuts
- croutons
- oyster crackers

SOMETHING BREADY
- toast soldiers
- sliced focaccia
- grilled cheese toasts

WHIP IT UP

PARMESAN BROTH

In a large pot, cover **leftover Parmesan rinds** with roughly 8 times their volume of **water**. Bring the mixture to a boil, then simmer it for an hour or two, until it's as flavorful as you like. Use immediately or let cool, then store in an airtight container in your fridge for up to 1 week or freeze for up to 3 months.

NOTES TO YOUR FUTURE SELF

MEATBALLS

_____
DOMINANT FLAVOR

& _____
CARB-Y BED

① Preheat the oven to 350°F.

② Place about 2 pounds of well-chilled ground _____ in a large
TYPE OF MEAT

bowl. If you're feeling frisky, throw in up to 1 cup chopped _____
CURED MEAT

on top. Beat 2 eggs and tip them into the bowl with a cup or so of _____ .
CRUMBS

Sprinkle about 1 teaspoon salt over everything.

③ With your bases covered, the rest is up to you: Add up to ½ cup each of finely chopped

raw or caramelized _____ , leftover cooked _____ ,
ALLIUMS   GRAINS

and/or _____ cheese, plus a couple tablespoons of minced
CRUMBLED OR GRATED CHEESE

_____ or _____ , a tablespoon
AROMATICS   FRESH HERBS

of _____ , and several pinches of _____ .
MORE FUN   SPICES

Live it up!

④ Rake your fingers through the bowl to help everything mingle without beating it up.

Shape the mixture between your palms into evenly sized balls (as small as a Ping-Pong

ball or as big as a peach) and keep 'em cold until you're ready to cook.

⑤ Pour a thin layer of oil into a heavy pan or Dutch oven and let it get hot over medium-

high heat. Add the meatballs and sear for just a couple of minutes per side, then tightly

cover the pan with foil and transfer it to the oven. Bake until the meatballs are cooked

through, 20 to 30 minutes. (If you've already got a _____ going
TYPE OF SAUCE

in a separate pot, you can skip the oven and add the seared meatballs directly to the

sauce to cook for 10 to 20 minutes. The choice is yours.)

⑥ Fill a wide bowl with _____ and a few meatballs, then drown it
CARB-Y BED

all with warmed sauce.

HINTS AND WINKS

DOMINANT FLAVOR
- spicy
- garlicky
- cheesy

CARB-Y BED
- **Baked Polenta**
- mashed potatoes
- cooked spaghetti
- risotto
- garlic bread

TYPE OF MEAT
- beef
- turkey
- lamb
- chicken
- sausage

CURED MEAT
- bacon or pancetta
- prosciutto
- salami

CRUMBS
- fine bread crumbs
- panko

ALLIUMS
- red, white, or yellow onion
- shallots
- garlic

GRAINS
- white or brown rice
- quinoa
- farro
- barley

CRUMBLED OR GRATED CHEESE
- Parmesan
- goat
- blue

AROMATICS
- garlic
- ginger or lemongrass
- citrus zest
- hot chiles

FRESH HERBS
- parsley
- cilantro
- oregano
- basil
- mint
- sage

MORE FUN
- soy sauce
- miso
- fish sauce
- tomato paste
- Worcestershire sauce
- Dijon mustard
- sesame oil
- sambal

SPICES
- smoked paprika
- fennel seeds
- red pepper flakes
- ground coriander or cumin
- curry or chili powder
- grated nutmeg

TYPE OF SAUCE
- marinara sauce
- gravy
- tahini sauce
- barbecue sauce
- pesto

BAKED POLENTA

With this dish, most of the work happens when you're not watching. For every **1 cup polenta,** use **4 cups water or stock,** and combine them in a large baking dish with **1 teaspoon salt** and a couple pinches of **spices** or a small heap of chopped **fresh herbs.** Bake at 350°F for 40 to 50 minutes, until it's tender and soft. Welcome it into this world by whisking in a few tablespoons of **butter or cream** and as much of your favorite **cheese** as your heart desires (plus a little more stock or water, if you want to thin it).

NOTES TO YOUR FUTURE SELF

_____

_____

_____

_____

_____ MEATBALLS
DOMINANT FLAVOR

& _____
CARB-Y BED

① Preheat the oven to 350°F.

② Place about 2 pounds of well-chilled ground _____ in a large
TYPE OF MEAT

bowl. If you're feeling frisky, throw in up to 1 cup chopped _____
CURED MEAT

on top. Beat 2 eggs and tip them into the bowl with a cup or so of _____ .
CRUMBS

Sprinkle about 1 teaspoon salt over everything.

③ With your bases covered, the rest is up to you: Add up to ½ cup each of finely chopped

raw or caramelized _____ , leftover cooked _____ ,
ALLIUMS   GRAINS

and/or _____ cheese, plus a couple tablespoons of minced
CRUMBLED OR GRATED CHEESE

_____ or _____ , a tablespoon
AROMATICS   FRESH HERBS

of _____ , and several pinches of _____ .
MORE FUN   SPICES

Live it up!

④ Rake your fingers through the bowl to help everything mingle without beating it up.

Shape the mixture between your palms into evenly sized balls (as small as a Ping-Pong

ball or as big as a peach) and keep 'em cold until you're ready to cook.

⑤ Pour a thin layer of oil into a heavy pan or Dutch oven and let it get hot over medium-

high heat. Add the meatballs and sear for just a couple of minutes per side, then tightly

cover the pan with foil and transfer it to the oven. Bake until the meatballs are cooked

through, 20 to 30 minutes. (If you've already got a _____ going
TYPE OF SAUCE

in a separate pot, you can skip the oven and add the seared meatballs directly to the

sauce to cook for 10 to 20 minutes. The choice is yours.)

⑥ Fill a wide bowl with _____ and a few meatballs, then drown it
CARB-Y BED

all with warmed sauce.

HINTS AND WINKS

DOMINANT FLAVOR
- spicy
- garlicky
- cheesy

CARB-Y BED
- **Baked Polenta**
- mashed potatoes
- cooked spaghetti
- risotto
- garlic bread

TYPE OF MEAT
- beef
- turkey
- lamb
- chicken
- sausage

CURED MEAT
- bacon or pancetta
- prosciutto
- salami

CRUMBS
- fine bread crumbs
- panko

ALLIUMS
- red, white, or yellow onion
- shallots
- garlic

GRAINS
- white or brown rice
- quinoa
- farro
- barley

CRUMBLED OR GRATED CHEESE
- Parmesan
- goat
- blue

AROMATICS
- garlic
- ginger or lemongrass
- citrus zest
- hot chiles

FRESH HERBS
- parsley
- cilantro
- oregano
- basil
- mint
- sage

MORE FUN
- soy sauce
- miso
- fish sauce
- tomato paste
- Worcestershire sauce
- Dijon mustard
- sesame oil
- sambal

SPICES
- smoked paprika
- fennel seeds
- red pepper flakes
- ground coriander or cumin
- curry or chili powder
- grated nutmeg

TYPE OF SAUCE
- marinara sauce
- gravy
- tahini sauce
- barbecue sauce
- pesto

WHIP IT UP

BAKED POLENTA

With this dish, most of the work happens when you're not watching. For every **1 cup polenta,** use **4 cups water or stock,** and combine them in a large baking dish with **1 teaspoon salt** and a couple pinches of **spices** or a small heap of chopped **fresh herbs**. Bake at 350°F for 40 to 50 minutes, until it's tender and soft. Welcome it into this world by whisking in a few tablespoons of **butter or cream** and as much of your favorite **cheese** as your heart desires (plus a little more stock or water, if you want to thin it).

NOTES TO YOUR FUTURE SELF

_____

_____

_____

_____

MEATBALLS

_____
DOMINANT FLAVOR

& _____
CARB-Y BED

① Preheat the oven to 350°F.

② Place about 2 pounds of well-chilled ground _____ in a large
TYPE OF MEAT

bowl. If you're feeling frisky, throw in up to 1 cup chopped _____
CURED MEAT

on top. Beat 2 eggs and tip them into the bowl with a cup or so of _____ .
CRUMBS

Sprinkle about 1 teaspoon salt over everything.

③ With your bases covered, the rest is up to you: Add up to ½ cup each of finely chopped

raw or caramelized _____ , leftover cooked _____ ,
ALLIUMS   GRAINS

and/or _____ cheese, plus a couple tablespoons of minced
CRUMBLED OR GRATED CHEESE

_____ or _____ , a tablespoon
AROMATICS   FRESH HERBS

of _____ , and several pinches of _____ .
MORE FUN   SPICES

Live it up!

④ Rake your fingers through the bowl to help everything mingle without beating it up.

Shape the mixture between your palms into evenly sized balls (as small as a Ping-Pong

ball or as big as a peach) and keep 'em cold until you're ready to cook.

⑤ Pour a thin layer of oil into a heavy pan or Dutch oven and let it get hot over medium-

high heat. Add the meatballs and sear for just a couple of minutes per side, then tightly

cover the pan with foil and transfer it to the oven. Bake until the meatballs are cooked

through, 20 to 30 minutes. (If you've already got a _____ going
TYPE OF SAUCE

in a separate pot, you can skip the oven and add the seared meatballs directly to the

sauce to cook for 10 to 20 minutes. The choice is yours.)

⑥ Fill a wide bowl with _____ and a few meatballs, then drown it
CARB-Y BED

all with warmed sauce.

HINTS AND WINKS

DOMINANT FLAVOR
- spicy
- garlicky
- cheesy

CARB-Y BED
- **Baked Polenta**
- mashed potatoes
- cooked spaghetti
- risotto
- garlic bread

TYPE OF MEAT
- beef
- turkey
- lamb
- chicken
- sausage

CURED MEAT
- bacon or pancetta
- prosciutto
- salami

CRUMBS
- fine bread crumbs
- panko

ALLIUMS
- red, white, or yellow onion
- shallots
- garlic

GRAINS
- white or brown rice
- quinoa
- farro
- barley

CRUMBLED OR GRATED CHEESE
- Parmesan
- goat
- blue

AROMATICS
- garlic
- ginger or lemongrass
- citrus zest
- hot chiles

FRESH HERBS
- parsley
- cilantro
- oregano
- basil
- mint
- sage

MORE FUN
- soy sauce
- miso
- fish sauce
- tomato paste
- Worcestershire sauce
- Dijon mustard
- sesame oil
- sambal

SPICES
- smoked paprika
- fennel seeds
- red pepper flakes
- ground coriander or cumin
- curry or chili powder
- grated nutmeg

TYPE OF SAUCE
- marinara sauce
- gravy
- tahini sauce
- barbecue sauce
- pesto

WHIP IT UP

BAKED POLENTA

With this dish, most of the work happens when you're not watching. For every **1 cup polenta,** use **4 cups water or stock,** and combine them in a large baking dish with **1 teaspoon salt** and a couple pinches of **spices** or a small heap of chopped **fresh herbs**. Bake at 350°F for 40 to 50 minutes, until it's tender and soft. Welcome it into this world by whisking in a few tablespoons of **butter or cream** and as much of your favorite **cheese** as your heart desires (plus a little more stock or water, if you want to thin it).

NOTES TO YOUR FUTURE SELF

_____

_____

_____

_____

_____ ENCHILADAS
ENTICING FILLING

WITH _____ SAUCE
RED OR GREEN

---

① Preheat the oven to 375°F.

② Start with the sauce: To make a red sauce, grab about 2 pounds tomatoes and a few

chipotles. For green sauce, start with about 2 pounds tomatillos, a couple of

_____ peppers, and maybe one or two _____ .
BIG, MILD GREEN PEPPERS   SPICY LI'L THINGS

Bonus points if you char your peppers under the broiler.

③ Blitz your sauce ingredients in a blender or food processor with ¼ to ½ cup chopped

_____ , a couple cloves of garlic, a little olive oil and lime juice,
ALLIUMS

and a few pinches of _____ , then cook in a skillet for 5 to
SPICES

10 minutes so everything thickens up a bit. Smudge a little sauce into the bottom of a

large baking dish.

④ Get a stack of small corn or flour tortillas, whichever you fancy. If they're not pliable,

soften them in a skillet with warm oil or wrap them in a damp paper towel and

microwave for 20-ish seconds. Dip them in the sauce to coat both sides, then fill each

one with a couple tablespoons of grated _____ cheese and
MELTY CHEESE

_____ . (Embrace the messiness.) Roll each tortilla snugly
ENTICING FILLING

around its filling and nestle them, side by side, seam down, in the baking dish. Once

they're all in there, drown them with the remaining sauce and top with an avalanche of

_____ . Bake until the cheesy top is freckled brown and the
SOMETHING TO GILD THE LILY

sauce beneath is bubbling away—about as long as it takes to drink a margarita.

⑤ Pile a serving into a bowl and top with _____ .
BITS & BOBS

HINTS AND WINKS

ENTICING FILLING
- shredded cooked chicken or pork
- sliced seared steak
- chopped cooked shrimp
- cooked or canned black beans
- leftover cooked vegetables

BIG, MILD GREEN PEPPERS
- bell
- poblano

SPICY LI'L THINGS
- jalapeños
- serranos
- habaneros

ALLIUMS
- white or red onions
- scallions

SPICES
- ground cumin or coriander
- chili powder
- achiote
- black pepper

MELTY CHEESE
- Monterey Jack
- pepper Jack
- cheddar

SOMETHING TO GILD THE LILY
- queso fresco
- cotija cheese
- more melty cheese

BITS & BOBS
- thinly sliced jalapeños
- radish matchsticks
- sprigs of cilantro
- crema
- guacamole
- pickled red onions
- lime wedges

TIP

SAUCY SHORTCUTS

Enchilada sauce is only as good as the vegetables you put into it, so if you can't get your hands on good fresh tomatoes or tomatillos, look to the canned-food aisle. One large can of **tomatoes** (approximately 28 ounces), puréed with one or two **canned chipotles in adobo sauce,** won't let you down. Same goes for **tomatillos,** if you can find them: spice them up with **canned Hatch chiles** or even a few **pickled jalapeños.**

NOTES TO YOUR FUTURE SELF

_____

_____

_____

_____

_____

_____

_____ ENCHILADAS
ENTICING FILLING

WITH _____ SAUCE
RED OR GREEN

① Preheat the oven to 375°F.

② Start with the sauce: To make a red sauce, grab about 2 pounds tomatoes and a few

chipotles. For green sauce, start with about 2 pounds tomatillos, a couple of

_____ peppers, and maybe one or two _____ .
BIG, MILD GREEN PEPPERS   SPICY LI'L THINGS

Bonus points if you char your peppers under the broiler.

③ Blitz your sauce ingredients in a blender or food processor with ¼ to ½ cup chopped

_____ , a couple cloves of garlic, a little olive oil and lime juice,
ALLIUMS

and a few pinches of _____ , then cook in a skillet for 5 to
SPICES

10 minutes so everything thickens up a bit. Smudge a little sauce into the bottom of a

large baking dish.

④ Get a stack of small corn or flour tortillas, whichever you fancy. If they're not pliable,

soften them in a skillet with warm oil or wrap them in a damp paper towel and

microwave for 20-ish seconds. Dip them in the sauce to coat both sides, then fill each

one with a couple tablespoons of grated _____ cheese and
MELTY CHEESE

_____ . (Embrace the messiness.) Roll each tortilla snugly
ENTICING FILLING

around its filling and nestle them, side by side, seam down, in the baking dish. Once

they're all in there, drown them with the remaining sauce and top with an avalanche of

_____ . Bake until the cheesy top is freckled brown and the
SOMETHING TO GILD THE LILY

sauce beneath is bubbling away—about as long as it takes to drink a margarita.

⑤ Pile a serving into a bowl and top with _____ .
BITS & BOBS

HINTS AND WINKS

ENTICING FILLING
- shredded cooked chicken or pork
- sliced seared steak
- chopped cooked shrimp
- cooked or canned black beans
- leftover cooked vegetables

BIG, MILD GREEN PEPPERS
- bell
- poblano

SPICY LI'L THINGS
- jalapeños
- serranos
- habaneros

ALLIUMS
- white or red onions
- scallions

SPICES
- ground cumin or coriander
- chili powder
- achiote
- black pepper

MELTY CHEESE
- Monterey Jack
- pepper Jack
- cheddar

SOMETHING TO GILD THE LILY
- queso fresco
- cotija cheese
- more melty cheese

BITS & BOBS
- thinly sliced jalapeños
- radish matchsticks
- sprigs of cilantro
- crema
- guacamole
- pickled red onions
- lime wedges

TIP

SAUCY SHORTCUTS

Enchilada sauce is only as good as the vegetables you put into it, so if you can't get your hands on good fresh tomatoes or tomatillos, look to the canned-food aisle. One large can of **tomatoes** (approximately 28 ounces), puréed with one or two **canned chipotles in adobo sauce,** won't let you down. Same goes for **tomatillos,** if you can find them: spice them up with **canned Hatch chiles** or even a few **pickled jalapeños.**

NOTES TO YOUR FUTURE SELF

_____

_____

_____

_____

_____

_____ ENCHILADAS
ENTICING FILLING

WITH _____ SAUCE
RED OR GREEN

① Preheat the oven to 375°F.

② Start with the sauce: To make a red sauce, grab about 2 pounds tomatoes and a few

chipotles. For green sauce, start with about 2 pounds tomatillos, a couple of

_____ peppers, and maybe one or two _____ .
BIG, MILD GREEN PEPPERS   SPICY LI'L THINGS

Bonus points if you char your peppers under the broiler.

③ Blitz your sauce ingredients in a blender or food processor with ¼ to ½ cup chopped

_____ , a couple cloves of garlic, a little olive oil and lime juice,
ALLIUMS

and a few pinches of _____ , then cook in a skillet for 5 to
SPICES

10 minutes so everything thickens up a bit. Smudge a little sauce into the bottom of a

large baking dish.

④ Get a stack of small corn or flour tortillas, whichever you fancy. If they're not pliable,

soften them in a skillet with warm oil or wrap them in a damp paper towel and

microwave for 20-ish seconds. Dip them in the sauce to coat both sides, then fill each

one with a couple tablespoons of grated _____ cheese and
MELTY CHEESE

_____ . (Embrace the messiness.) Roll each tortilla snugly
ENTICING FILLING

around its filling and nestle them, side by side, seam down, in the baking dish. Once

they're all in there, drown them with the remaining sauce and top with an avalanche of

_____ . Bake until the cheesy top is freckled brown and the
SOMETHING TO GILD THE LILY

sauce beneath is bubbling away—about as long as it takes to drink a margarita.

⑤ Pile a serving into a bowl and top with _____ .
BITS & BOBS

HINTS AND WINKS

ENTICING FILLING
- shredded cooked chicken or pork
- sliced seared steak
- chopped cooked shrimp
- cooked or canned black beans
- leftover cooked vegetables

BIG, MILD GREEN PEPPERS
- bell
- poblano

SPICY LI'L THINGS
- jalapeños
- serranos
- habaneros

ALLIUMS
- white or red onions
- scallions

SPICES
- ground cumin or coriander
- chili powder
- achiote
- black pepper

MELTY CHEESE
- Monterey Jack
- pepper Jack
- cheddar

SOMETHING TO GILD THE LILY
- queso fresco
- cotija cheese
- more melty cheese

BITS & BOBS
- thinly sliced jalapeños
- radish matchsticks
- sprigs of cilantro
- crema
- guacamole
- pickled red onions
- lime wedges

TIP
SAUCY SHORTCUTS

Enchilada sauce is only as good as the vegetables you put into it, so if you can't get your hands on good fresh tomatoes or tomatillos, look to the canned-food aisle. One large can of **tomatoes** (approximately 28 ounces), puréed with one or two **canned chipotles in adobo sauce,** won't let you down. Same goes for **tomatillos,** if you can find them: spice them up with **canned Hatch chiles** or even a few **pickled jalapeños**.

NOTES TO YOUR FUTURE SELF

_____

_____

_____

_____

_____

ACKNOWLEDGMENTS

Rémy Robert, thank you for your warm, witty, and all-around-delicious writing—not to mention your recipes, which make us want to lick the last drop from every spoon. Sarah Jampel, thank you for bringing this clever concept to life, one of many you've made sparkle at Food52 over the years. You are the ketchup to our fries. Tim McSweeney, thank you for your illustrations that bring whimsy and imagination to everything from salad to pasta squiggles. Suzanne D'Amato, Kristen Miglore, Alexis Anthony, Joanna Sciarrino, and Brinda Ayer—thank you for your masterful cat herding and commitment to making this new endeavor the best it can be. Thanks also to Amanda Englander, our fearless editor; Kari Stuart, our whip-smart agent; and the team at Clarkson Potter for working tirelessly to help us perfect each scribble and soup bowl. Now, let's all have some snacks.

—Amanda Hesser & Merrill Stubbs, co-founders